Build Your Business Grammar

Tim Bowen

Language Teaching Publications
114a Church Road, Hove, BN3 2EB, England
Tel: 00 44 (1) 273 736344
Fax: 00 44 (1) 273 775361

ISBN 1 899396 45 4
© LTP 1997
Reprinted 1999

The Author
Tim Bowen is a teacher and teacher trainer at International House, Hastings, where he is Director of the Business English Centre. He is responsible for the production of business-orientated materials within the school. He has taught English and trained teachers in a number of countries and is co-author of *The Pronunciation Book* (Longman) and *Inside Teaching* (Heinemann). He is an enthusiastic supporter of the Lexical Approach and his current interests in the field of language teaching include contrastive linguistics and etymology.

Acknowledgements
Cover design by Anna Macleod
Cover photograph courtesy of The Stock Market
Illustrations and additional material by Jon Marks
Typesetting by Sean M. Worsfold
Printed in England by Commercial Colour Press Plc, London E7

INTRODUCTION

THE GRAMMAR OF BUSINESS ENGLISH

The grammar of a language is the structure of its key concepts. The grammar of business English is a wider idea than traditional grammar. Not only does it include ideas such as *the present perfect* or *modals*, it also includes ideas such as *advising, agreeing, negotiating*. This book practises business grammar in this wider sense.

WHAT IS THIS BOOK?

Build Your Business Grammar is a practice book which covers most key structures in a business context. Each unit is based on a typical situation found in the world of business and focuses on the key language likely to be used in such situations. The example sentences used in the exercises are usually part of an extended dialogue, letter, fax or report and thus provide a complete context, rather than being isolated, unconnected examples. The situations used in the book represent typical areas of business communication such as telephoning, meetings, negotiations, and reports.

WHO IS THIS BOOK FOR?

This book is for learners of English working in the general area of business and commerce at an intermediate level. It will be useful for learners wishing to extend their vocabulary as well as for those wishing to practise particular structures in a business context.

SHOULD I START AT THE BEGINNING?

You do not need to work through the units systematically in chronological order. It is better to concentrate on those areas which interest you most – those which are most appropriate to your own area of business, and those which cover the areas of grammar and vocabulary which present you with the most problems.

CAN I USE THIS BOOK AT HOME?

You can use this book for self-study or in class with a teacher. The exercises are particularly suitable as homework, which may then be checked in class with your teacher. There is a key to all the exercises. Key words and phrases are recycled throughout the book and some units contain exercises which encourage you to underline or otherwise highlight such words and expressions.

Working through **Build Your Business Grammar** will give you lots of practice in the use of many basic English structures, as well as helping you to learn a wide range of vocabulary, phrases and idioms in current use.

CONTENTS

Section 1   Everyday Business English

Section 2   Problem Solving

Section 3   Business Travel

Section 4   Facts and Figures

Section 5   Presentations

Section 6   Phone and Fax

Section 7   Reports

Section 8   Meetings and Negotiations

Section 1
Everyday Business English

Unit 1.1 It's too late.
Language focus – *there (be)* and *it (be)*

EXERCISE 1

Complete these with *there* or *it* and part of the verb *(be)*.

1. . . . . too late; . . . . nothing we can do about it now.
2. . . . . not my fault. . . . . proper ways to do things and you didn't follow the procedure.
3. . . . . problems when the news gets out. . . . . not the right way to introduce an important change in the way we work.
4. . . . . time to go. If we leave now, ... time to call in at Head Office on the way to the airport.
5. . . . . a vacancy in the Accounts Department. . . . . for someone to control the accounts of the dozen or so major clients.
6. . . . . a nuisance but . . . . nothing we can do from our end. We'll just have to wait.
7. . . . . gate 57, but . . . . still time for the duty free shop!
8. . . . . problems with the fax machine which we need to get fixed and . . . . urgent.
   > Right, I'll ring straightaway. . . . . no time like the present.
9. We've run out of headed paper.
   > I think . . . . a couple of boxes in the stationery cupboard.
10. . . . . been a big change in the exchange rate. . . . . now nearly 3DM to the pound.
11. . . . . only a couple of days before the deadline, so . . . . a top priority.
12. . . . . no point in worrying about it. . . . . too late.

Now add *there's* or *it's* to the following short expressions:

13. . . . . too late / not my fault / time to go / a nuisance / a priority.
14. . . . . still time / no point in waiting / nothing we can do / problems / no time like the present.

EXERCISE 2

Where do you think each of the examples above was used? Mark them:

   O – for the office   M – for a meeting   T – for travelling

1.	4.	7.	10. . . . .
2.	5.	8.	11. . . . .
3.	6.	9.	12. . . . .

Unit 1.2 Too much Trouble
Language focus – *much* and *many*

EXERCISE 1

1. Two of the following words can be used with *much*, but never with *many*.
2. Two can be used (in the plural of course) with *many* but never with *much*.
3. Four can be used with *much*.   4. Four can be used with *many*.

| money | customer | time | trouble |
| change | development | opportunity | account |

1. much . . . . much . . . .
2. many . . . . many . . . .
3. much . . . . much . . . .   much . . . .   much . . . .
4. many . . . . many . . . .   many . . . .   many . . . .

EXERCISE 2

Now use one of the expressions to complete each of these.

1. They're very helpful. Nothing is too . . . . for them.
2. It's never a good idea to make too . . . . at one time. It's better to take things step-by-step.
3. There aren't as . . . . in the former Eastern European countries as many business people seem to think.
4. There have been so . . . . since our last meeting that I'd better begin by summarising the present position.
5. Too . . . . is wasted on planning projects which never actually happen.
6. Not too . . . . know this, so keep it to yourself, but she's already handed in her resignation.

EXERCISE 3

Often we use other words with *much* and *many* to give a more precise picture. Complete these expressions using each of these once:

| great | as | nowhere | all |
| good | too (x2) | far | |

1. . . . . too many.
2. not . . . . much as I expected.
3. not . . . . that much.
4. a . . . . many people.
5. a . . . . many more than we first thought.
6. . . . . near as much as that.
7. How many mistakes did I make?
   > . . . . many!
8. How much did you lose?
   > . . . . much!

Unit 1.3　Office Talk 1
Language focus – the *'ll* future

EXERCISE 1

Read the sentences below. Decide which of the following uses of *will* / *'ll* best fits each sentence.

> a. an opinion about the future
> b. a promise or undertaking
> c. a request

1. Do you think sales will improve next month?
2. I'll phone you again tomorrow.
3. Will you ring me again and give me the details?
4. It looks as if the shipment will be late again this month.
5. It's OK. I'll do it later.
6. I don't think this plan will work.
7. Just sign these letters for me, will you?
8. What do you think will happen next month?
9. I'll finish it by tomorrow morning.
10. I'll try and bring the documentation tomorrow.

EXERCISE 2

Now rewrite these sentences containing *will* in the correct order. If the sentence is a promise or undertaking, you need to use *'ll*, rather than *will*.

1. you will cost know how do much it?

. . . .

2. think contract they when do will sign you the?

. . . .

3. details you fax soon back the with we as possible as will

. . . .

4. phone I and tomorrow again try will

. . . .

5. you plan do be think the when will ready draft?

. . . .

6. take the long it finish to project will how?

. . . .

7. further send later you I details will

. . . .

8. confirm possible please soon you will this as as?

. . . .

GRAMMAR NOTE

Will is not normally used for arrangements in the future which are already fixed. In such cases, the present continuous is usually used. For example:
I'm sorry I can't come tomorrow. I'm meeting an important client at 11.30.

Unit 1.4   Office Talk 2
Language focus – *would*

EXERCISE 1

Read the sentences below. Decide which of the following uses of *would* best fits each sentence:

> a. past habit
> b. refusal
> c. hypothetical or conditional situation
> d. polite request or offer
> e. past form of *will* – especially in reported speech

1. We would be very happy to send you further information.   . . . . . .
2. He would often spend the entire weekend at the office.   . . . . . .
3. Would you let us know your decision at your earliest convenience?. . . . . .
4. In that situation we wouldn't be able to hold the price down.   . . . . . .
5. She said she would phone again tomorrow.   . . . . . .
6. Occasionally he would work late into the night.   . . . . . .
7. Would you fill in this form, please?   . . . . . .
8. Life would be much easier if we had better equipment.   . . . . . .
9. I'm afraid they wouldn't agree to our terms.   . . . . . .
10. They told us they would let us know soon.   . . . . . .
11. Would you like some more coffee?   . . . . . .
12. The problem was that they wouldn't accept any changes   . . . . . .
    to the contract.

EXERCISE 2

Now rewrite the following sentences. They are the words of a negotiator reporting what happened at a meeting:

1. agree I'm they price the increase wouldn't afraid to

. . . .

2. the renegotiate they they to contract said would prefer

. . . .

3. would better a also be new us agreement for

. . . .

4. chance it terms give would the to us negotiate new

. . . .

5. insert able we be to a penalty would clause

. . . .

GRAMMAR NOTE

Would can be used to express past habits – *He would often arrive at the office late.* Used to is, however, more common – *He often used to arrive at the office late.* Notice the position of *often* in these examples.

Unit 1.5 Work Routines
Language focus – present simple, adverbials of time

EXERCISE 1

The adverbial is in the wrong place in all these examples. Rewrite them correctly.

1. I every day receive as many as a hundred faxes.

. . . .

2. Also I have to send a lot of faxes.

. . . .

3. This takes up a lot of time usually.

. . . .

4. Never I have enough time for all the work I have to do.

. . . .

5. But I very much like my job.

. . . .

6. I meet people from different countries often.

. . . .

7. As well I have to travel abroad a lot.

. . . .

8. I about once a month fly to North America.

. . . .

EXERCISE 2

This is a description of the meetings held in a particular company. Rewrite the sentences in an appropriate order:

1. meeting have a a board we month once

. . . .

2. place this boardroom in the takes

. . . .

3. attend board meetings members always these

. . . .

4. usually spend matters most financial we time on

. . . .

5. rarely sales these are marketing at meetings discussed and

. . . .

6. left matters such are departmental to meetings generally

. . . .

7. are held on normally weekly these Fridays

. . . .

8. also we have meetings often management fairly

. . . .

12

Unit 1.6   Business Idioms 1
Language focus – prepositional phrases

EXERCISE 1

Complete the prepositional phrases below by adding, one of the following prepositions from the list:

wide of   *under*   *across*   *in*   *to*   *out of*   *on*

1. . . . . the same boat
2. . . . . the ball
3. . . . . the dot
4. . . . . the pipeline
5. . . . . his depth

6. . . . . the mark
7. . . . . the board
8. . . . . touch
9. . . . . the letter
10. . . . . wraps

EXERCISE 2

Now complete the sentences below using the prepositional phrases above:

1. The 5% increase will be applied . . . . , so everyone will benefit.
2. It starts at 11 o'clock . . . . , so don't be late!
3. We're all . . . . Everyone'll be affected by the economy drive.
4. She's very well informed. She's really . . . .
5. Her colleague, however, seems to have problems understanding what's going on. He's . . . . in this kind of discussion.
6. Customs regulations have to be followed . . . .
7. The whole idea is still . . . . for the time being, so don't tell anyone about it.
8. There are a number of new products . . . . and we hope to have them ready early in the New Year.
9. He's been away from the office for so long that he's really . . . . with what's going on here.
10. Your estimates for the cost of the project were a long way . . . . It cost more than twice as much as you thought it would.

GRAMMAR NOTE

There are a lot of commonly used idiomatic prepositional phrases like these in English. It is important to try and learn them as whole expressions, rather than just the noun, for example. One way of recording such expressions is to list them under the preposition. For example:

IN   > *in the same boat, in the pipeline, in a nutshell*

Unit 1.7   Business Idioms 2
Language focus – prepositional phrases

EXERCISE 1

Complete the prepositional phrases by adding a suitable preposition. Choose from:

| at | below | from | in | off | on | out of |

1. . . . . . . scratch
2. . . . . . . the question
3. . . . . . . cross purposes
4. . . . . . . par
5. . . . . . . the record
6. . . . . . . a nutshell
7. . . . . . . the balance
8. . . . . . . odds
9. . . . . . . a rut
10. . . . . . . thin ice

EXERCISE 2

Now complete the following using the above expressions:

1. We are not satisfied with his work. His recent performance has been . . . . , I'm afraid.
2. This report is useless. We'll have to do it all again . . . .
3. I think we're talking . . . . here. I'm talking about one thing and you're talking about a completely different matter.
4. I'm sorry, that's . . . . It's completely unacceptable as far as we are concerned.
5. The situation is rather dangerous. We're . . . . here and I don't know what's going to happen.
6. They are. . . . . with us about the payment clause and it's going to be very difficult to resolve our differences.
7. I'm . . . . in this job. I need a fresh challenge.
8. I won't go into details at the moment, but . . . . , the company is in serious trouble.
9. We still haven't been informed officially, but . . . . we've got the Chinese contract.
10. This week will be crucial. The whole future of this company is . . . .

GRAMMAR NOTE

Remember it is important to learn the **whole** expression. Here is an example. Can you add more to each line?

IN	. . . . *in the same boat, in the pipeline, in a nutshell* . . . .
OUT	. . . .
AT	. . . .
ON	. . . .

14

Unit 1.8 Business Idioms 3
Language focus – prepositional phrases

EXERCISE 1

Complete these prepositional phrases:

    at   *in*   *for*   *by*   *out of*   *on*   *to*

1. . . . . . . connection with
2. . . . . . . first sight
3. . . . . . . other words
4. . . . . . . the long run
5. . . . . . . a change
6. . . . . . . the dark
7. . . . . . . the deep end
8. . . . . . . the time being
9. . . . . . . the blue
10. . . . . . . a guess
11. . . . . . . chance
12. . . . . . . equal terms
13. . . . . . . the wrong foot
14. . . . . . . the whole

EXERCISE 2

Now complete the following using the above expressions:

1. I met him quite . . . . We were waiting to check in at Heathrow Airport and he was in the next queue. I had no idea he was travelling on the same flight.
2. I'm not absolutely sure but, ... , I would say that there are about 2,500 people working there.
3. The news of the closure of the factory came . . . . No one was expecting it to happen.
4. I am writing . . . . your advertisement in the Financial Times of Friday, August 27th.
5. We have to participate . . . . in this project. Both sides should have the same conditions and benefits.
6. . . . . , this proposal doesn't seem very promising, but if you read it carefully, it has a lot of potential.
7. We always fly to Paris. Why don't we use the Channel Tunnel . . . . ?
8. We have to economise – . . . . , we have to save money wherever and whenever we can.
9. The short-term prospects are not good, but . . . . I think this project will be a good one.
10. I think you'd better stay in the Paris office . . . . , but next year we'll probably transfer you to New York.
11. Everyone is completely . . . . No one has any idea what's happening.
12. We were caught . . . . when they asked for delivery before June 30th.
13. I agree . . . . , but I still have some reservations.
14. I had no preparation – they just threw me in . . . . with one of the most important accounts in Europe.

15

Unit 1.9   Some Useful Information

Language focus – countable and uncountable nouns

Choose the correct alternative in each of the following sentences:

1. We would be grateful for your a) advice / b) advices on this matter.

2. Thank you for the a) information / b) informations concerning the schedule.

3. Could you supply the usual bank and trade a) reference? / b) references?

4. Please accept our sincere a) apology / b) apologies for the delay.

5. We have excellent storage a) facility. / b) facilities.

6. The annual a) account / b) accounts must be submitted not later than January 31st.

7. We close our a) book / b) books for the financial year on June 30.

8. We won't make a profit, but at least it will make a contribution to a) overhead. / b) overheads.

9. I understand they are in a) debt / b) debts at the moment.

10. Let us have a note of your a) expense / b) expenses as soon as you get back.

11. We have no a) knowledge / b) knowledges of the proposal to increase import duty.

12. We have made substantial a) progress / b) progresses since we last spoke to you.

GRAMMAR NOTE

Some nouns which are plural in some other languages are not used in the plural in English; the most useful in business English are *advice, information, knowledge.*

Notice many nouns have both countable and uncountable uses, depending on exactly what the speaker has in mind; often the plural is used for particular examples and the uncountable for the idea in general:

Too many regulations from Brussels are bad for business.
Too much regulation from Brussels is bad for business.

16

Unit 1.10   Instructions and Suggestions
Language focus – negative imperative

EXERCISE 1

Complete the following with one of these words plus *don't* or *do not*.

    miss   *obstruct*   *use*   *enter*   *delay*

    forget (x2)   *worry*   *mention*   *expect*

1. . . . . the meeting tomorrow. It starts at 8.30.
2. . . . . – write today and receive a free gift if your reply is received by June 30.
3. . . . . to include a stamped addressed envelope with your reply.
4. . . . . the delay unless they actually ask about it.
5. . . . . these gates. Access needed at all times.
6. . . . . to get an order today – they always send their orders two or three days later by fax.
7. . . . . the chance of a free holiday – act today!
8. . . . . without protective clothing.
9. . . . . in the event of fire.
10. . . . . , it's only ten to. We'll be there with time to spare.

EXERCISE 2

Put the above into three groups. Those from sales letters (L), those from public notices (N), and those from something you might say to a colleague (S):

L   . . . .

N   . . . .

S   . . . .

GRAMMAR NOTE

When you are stopping or prohibiting something, you use *do not;* when you are encouraging or suggesting, you use *don't*. Look back at the examples above and check whether you have used *don't* and *do not* in the correct way.

Don't ask me, I only work here.

Unit 1.11   A Range of Colours
Language focus – expressions with *of*

You know expressions like *a bottle of beer*, and *a can of Coke*, but how many of these similar expressions which are common in business do you know? Complete each sentence with two words, one from List 1 and one from List 2.

LIST 1		LIST 2	
pace	range	spare parts	luck
stroke	flood	satisfaction	income
shadow	level	colours	confidence
lack	loss	complaints	doubt
shortage	rate	development	growth

1. All the clothes in the summer collection are available in a . . . . of . . . . , though we expect yellow and turquoise to be the two most popular.

2. We'll get the contract – it'll take a few weeks before they decide but I don't think there's a . . . . of a . . . . that we'll get it.

3. Problems in the production department have been caused by a . . . . of . . . . which has meant we have not been able to repair machines as quickly as we usually do.

4. We're looking for a . . . . of . . . . in Eastern European sales of at least 20%.

5. There was a strike which meant we couldn't service orders to Europe and that meant a serious . . . . of . . . . during July. We were 35% under budget for that month.

6. Nobody is buying, and nobody is selling. There's a serious . . . . of . . . . in the economy at the moment.

7. Things are still ticking over but the . . . . of . . . . has slowed considerably in the last few months.

8. The AX7 was launched too soon, without adequate testing, and within days we had a . . . . of . . . . about the doors which simply weren't secure. We were lucky there wasn't a serious accident.

9. Our market survey shows consumers reported the highest . . . . of . . . . we have ever had in the first weeks after the launch of the new range. We're delighted with the positive reaction.

10. We had a real . . . . of . . . . when we got to Tokyo – they'd just appointed a new chief buyer and he was an old friend of Jack's from his time with Phillips in Osaka.

Unit 1.12   A Waste of Time
Language focus – more expressions with *of*

EXERCISE 1

Choose one word from each list to complete the following sentences. Look again at Unit 1.11 and notice expressions like *level of satisfaction*.

LIST 1		LIST 2	
window	*token*	*interests*	*time*
time	*error*	*judgement*	*payment*
team	*date*	*opportunity*	*despatch*
member	*waste*	*goodwill*	*arrival*
method	*portfolio*	*experts*	*staff*

1. It's a complete . . . . of . . . . seeing them – they promise everything and never order anything.
2. If you let me know your expected . . . . of . . . . , I'll try to pick you up at the airport.
3. If I can't be at the airport myself, a . . . . of my . . . . will be there to meet you.
4. We apologise for the inconvenience and as a . . . . of . . . . we enclose a voucher for $100 which may be used at any of our hotels or restaurants.
5. You shouldn't have told them about the problems we're having. That was a serious . . . . of . . . . on your part.
6. If you could confirm the . . . . of . . . . from your warehouse, this information will help us trace the consignment.
7. We can issue a pro forma invoice but the most convenient . . . . of . . . . for you is almost certainly using a credit card.
8. We are doing everything we can to trace the source of the problem and we have called in a . . . . of outside . . . . to help.
9. There's a . . . . of . . . . if we act now, before our competitors hear what's happening.
10. He doesn't believe in keeping all his eggs in one basket, so he has a very wide . . . . of . . . . – everything from garages to food, from office equipment to a travel agency.

EXERCISE 2

Which word does *not* make a strong partnership with the word in capitals? Make sure you know all the other expressions in your own language.

1. FLOOD of *complaints   money   applications   danger   enquiries   orders*
2. FLOW of *information   money   ideas   time   people   support*

Notice words which are used to talk about how water moves (*flow, flood*) are also used for many other things. Rearrange these letters to make other verbs which are used with *water*, but also with *money, information*, etc. Can you do the same in your own language?

3. CEIKLRT. . . . .   AEMRST . . . .   EIDT . . . .

Unit 1.13   More Office Talk 1
Language focus – expressions with *have*

Use the words given to fill the gaps in the sentences:

appointment	day off	headache	holiday	go
disagreement	meeting	idea	conversation	chance
difficulty	the steak	alternative	break	doubt
time (x 2)	look	word	business	

1. Do you think you could have a . . . . at these figures?
2. We had a major . . . . about the financial arrangements.
3. I have an important . . . . at 3 o'clock.
4. We have no . . . . We have to agree.
5. Can I have a . . . . with you, please? It's about the new contract.
6. I had a lot of . . . . understanding some of the details in this document.
7. Did you have a good . . . . ? How did the meeting go?
8. Good morning. I have an . . . . with the Manager at 11 o'clock.
9. Shall we have a five-minute . . . . ?
10. You look rather tired. Why don't you have a . . . . tomorrow?
11. I had a very interesting . . . . with the Financial Director on the plane.
12. Did you have a good . . . . ? You look as if you got plenty of sun.
13. She had a brilliant . . . . yesterday. It could save us a lot of money.
14. I'm sorry I wasn't at the meeting yesterday. I had a terrible . . . .
15. Sorry! I didn't have . . . . to read all the stuff last night.
16. He's very successful. He's had his own . . . . for years.
17. I think I'll have . . . . with pepper sauce. It's a while since I had one.
18. I can't get this machine to work. Do you think you could have a . . . . . . ?
19. Have you had a . . . . to look at those figures yet?
20. I have no . . . . at all that things will sort themselves out.

Go back and underline all the expressions which contain the verb *have*. Make sure you know the equivalent in your own language.

GRAMMAR NOTE

The verb *have* does not carry much meaning in any of the above examples; the nouns which follow carry most of the meaning. It is important to learn expressions like these as complete expressions – *to have a good time.*

Unit 1.14   More Office Talk 2
Language focus – phrasal verbs with *get*

EXERCISE 1

Some phrasal verbs are often used in a business context. Complete the following sentences using the following words:

across	*through*	*on with*	*by*	*back to*
down to	*together*	*round*	*over*	*at*

1. She is very easy to get . . . . She is open, friendly and easy-going.
2. It is extremely important that we get this message . . . . . . clearly. There must be no misunderstandings whatsoever.
3. It will probably take a very long time for the company to get . . . . . . its current difficulties. The recovery might not take place until next year.
4. Right, ladies and gentlemen. It's time to start. Let's get . . . . . . business.
5. I tried calling our office in Geneva several times, but I couldn't get . . . . . .
6. I'm very sorry. I don't have that information to hand at the moment. I'll get . . . . . . you later, if I may.
7. Sometimes it is very difficult to get . . . . . . customs regulations in certain countries.
8. Right, we will need to get . . . . . . again next week to discuss the contract in more detail.
9. I'm sorry, I don't understand. What exactly are you getting . . . . . . ?
10. In these recessionary times, many small businesses are finding it very difficult to get . . . .

EXERCISE 2

Now match the verbs used with their meanings. Make sure you know the equivalent in your own language.

1. to get (a message) across	a. to avoid
2. to get at	b. to meet each other
3. to get back to (someone)	c. to recover from
4. to get by	d. to telephone later
5. to get down to (business)	e. to communicate
6. to get on with someone	f. to co-exist / co-operate successfully
7. to get over	g. to get a telephone connection
8. to get round (regulations etc)	h. to begin serious work / discussion
9. to get through	i. to mean (see Note below)
10. to get together	j. to survive

GRAMMAR NOTE

Get at in the sense of *mean* is generally used in the expressions: *What are you getting at?* or *What I'm getting at is . . .* or *I don't know what they were getting at.* It is normally used in the continuous form.

Unit 1.15 Doing Business, Making Money
Language focus – *do* and *make*

EXERCISE 1

Put the appropriate part of *do* or *make* in the following:

1. We . . . . a lot of business with the Third World.
2. I think I ought to . . . . an appointment.
3. I don't want to . . . . difficulties, but it is very short notice.
4. I . . . . a number of useful contacts at the Fair.
5. We . . . . progress but it's a long job.
6. If we don't . . . . much of a profit, at least we won't . . . . a loss.
7. We need someone to . . . . the cleaning.
8. You can't . . . . business without taking risks.
9. I can never . . . . any work on the plane.
10. I think they . . . . a special weekend price. It's worth asking.
11. It looks as if someone has . . . . a silly mistake on this invoice.
12. It . . . . a lot of damage to their reputation.
13. We'd be delighted to . . . . the job for you.
14. Their factory . . . . a very poor impression on me.
15. I'll . . . . enquiries for you and get back to you later today.
16. We'll have to . . . . something about it. We ought to . . . . a complaint.
17. We've . . . . a lot of work, but we haven't . . . . much progress.
18. Somebody has definitely . . . . a mistake. Now, what are you going to . . . . about it?

Underline all the expressions which contain *do* or *make*.

EXERCISE 2

Complete all of these fixed phrases with either *do* or *make*.

1. . . . . an appointment
2. . . . . the post
3. . . . . a mess
4. . . . . your best
5. . . . . a note of it
6. . . . . well
7. . . . . everything we can to help
8. . . . . yourself understood
9. . . . . something about it

Which of these expressions will be useful to you in your job? Make sure you know the equivalents in your own language.

Section 2
Problem Solving

Unit 2.1 Problems in the Office
Language focus – fixed expressions

What are the people in the pictures saying? Use each of these expressions once:

a. *I can't get through.*
b. *I'm afraid we're out of stock.*
c. *Sorry.*
d. *What's the matter?*
e. *Whoops!*

f. *I think it's crashed.*
g. *It's jammed.*
h. *What a mess!*
i. *What's the problem?*
j. *Would you mind not doing that?*

1. . . . .

2. . . . .

3. . . . .

4. . . . .

5. . . . . 6. . . . .

7. . . . . 8. . . . .

9. . . . . 10. . . . .

Unit 2.2   Minor Problems
Language focus – 'll and the present perfect simple

EXERCISE 1

Complete the sentences below using the present perfect of one of these verbs:

miss	*come out*	*mislay*	*run out of*
arrive	*jam*	*forget*	*change*

1. I . . . . the price list you sent me.
2. The photocopier . . . . again.
3. I don't think the post . . . . yet, has it?
4. These copies . . . . very well.
5. I'm sorry. I . . . . .to bring the report.
6. I think I . . . . the last train home.
7. They . . . . their fax number, I think.
8. We . . . . photocopy paper.

EXERCISE 2

Complete the solutions to each of the problems above by using one of the following verbs in these sentences:

get	*send*	*see*	*give (x2)*	*run off*	*order*	*check*

a. They have. I'll . . . . you their new one.
b. It's OK. I'll . . . . some more for you.
c. Don't worry. I'll . . . . you another one.
d. I'll . . . . you a lift if you like.
e. I'll . . . . some more today.
f. I'll . . . . and see if it's here.
g. I'll . . . . if I can fix it. The paper's probably jammed.
h. Don't worry. I'll . . . . a copy from someone else.

EXERCISE 3

Now match the problems and solutions:

1	2	3	4	5	6	7	8

GRAMMAR NOTE

To report a problem that has just happened, use the present perfect – *I've forgotten my key*. To offer help use *'ll* + infinitive: *It's all right. I'll lend you mine.*

26

Unit 2.3   Bad News
Language focus – adjectives

EXERCISE 1

We often express a negative idea by using *not very* + (positive equivalent):

The results were bad. > The results weren't very good.

Change these in the same way:

1. Their machinery is old-fashioned.

. . . .

2. Their order processing is slow.

. . . .

3. The catalogue is very dull.

. . . .

4. We got rather a cool reception.

. . . .

5. We are dissatisfied with the service we have received so far.

. . . .

6. We're unhappy with some of the terms of the proposed agreement.

. . . .

You will need to change these in a similar, but not exactly the same, way:

7. We made very little money on the deal.

. . . .

8. He takes no interest in what we do.

. . . .

9. There's no alternative. (many other options)

. . . .

10. There's nothing we can do about it.

. . . .

Do you do the same thing in your language or do you always say things very directly?

EXERCISE 2

Rewrite the words given to make a sentence with a similar meaning to the one given.

1. I've lost them.
   I at hand put on them moment can't the my

. . . .

2. I don't agree.
   I agree you there can't with quite

. . . .

3. We don't want one.
   We really at not moment are the interested

. . . .

Unit 2.4   Not the Usual Routine
Language focus – present simple and continuous

Complete each of these sentences with the correct forms of the verb given in brackets.

1. It normally . . . . about two weeks, but this one . . . . longer than usual. *(take)*

2. We usually . . . . everything by post, but we . . . . this package by courier so we can track it if there are any problems. *(send)*

3. The company usually . . . . us business class tickets, but they . . . . us economy tickets for this trip because there are so many of us going. *(give)*

4. We normally . . . . a London firm but we . . . . somebody local this time so we can keep an eye on every detail. *(use)*

5. Typically we . . . . prices once a year, from January the first, but this time we . . . . the dollar prices immediately because of the big change in the exchange rate. *(increase)*

6. We . . . . a couple of hundred pounds on gifts every Christmas, but this is our tenth anniversary, so we . . . . a good deal more this year. *(spend)*

7. We always . . . . to keep firm control over expenses, but in the present climate we . . . . even harder than we usually do. *(try)*

8. We don't . . . . more than we need at the best of times, and we . . . . a penny more than we need with interest rates at 12%. *(borrow)*

Grammar Note

Look at the verbs in the examples again. All follow the same pattern. Can you make a rule for yourself?
The present simple describes the **general** situation (what *usually, regularly, normally* happens) and the present continuous often refers to a **particular** situation.

28

Unit 2.5   Computer Problems
Language focus – necessity

EXERCISE 1

When you want to say what is necessary to solve a problem you often use
'll have to:

>   We're snowed under with orders at the moment.
>   > *You'll have to* take on some temporary help.

Advise me what to do when my computer has these problems. (Try to do this first without looking at the helpful ideas at the bottom of the page.)

1. The memory is full.

. . . .

2. Nothing happens when I move the mouse.

. . . .

3. My computer is rather old and slow.

. . . .

4. I can't find the information I need in the manual.

. . . .

5. I'm doing an important job which will take several days.

. . . .

EXERCISE 2

Make full sentences using the words given; you also need *have to, must* or *mustn't* in each case.

1. You/forget/back up the file.

. . . .

2. You/remember/save changes.

. . . .

3. You/load/new version/before/works.

. . . .

4. You/use/until/new version/loaded.

. . . .

5. You/overload/memory/opening too many files.

. . . .

GRAMMAR NOTE

have to is used to say what is absolutely necessary because of the law or some **external** reason – *You have to close the database before you can open the wordprocessor package.*

must and *'ll have to* are similar; they say what **the speaker** thinks you need to do – *You'll have to turn it off, and re-boot.*

(Ideas for Exercise 1: delete some files; re-boot; upgrade the whole system; helpline; back up the file every evening.)

Unit 2.6   More Problems
Language focus – advice

EXERCISE 1

First complete each of the solution expressions using one of these words or phrases. Then match each problem with a possible solution.

> *why don't*   *could try*   *time*   *have to*
> *what about*   *strongly advise*   *were*   *you'd better*

PROBLEMS

1. This fund isn't performing very well.
2. The photocopier's out of order again.
3. I can't get through to the Paris office. I've been trying all morning.
4. There's a problem with your Madrid flight. Apparently, it's fully booked.
5. I've got a client coming to see me at 4 pm, but we've got a meeting then.
6. I've got to get these documents to the London office by 4pm at the latest.
7. We still haven't received any payments since July.
8. This fax is completely illegible.

SOLUTIONS

a. . . . . you re-schedule your trip for next week?
b. You'll . . . . call them and ask them to send it again.
c. . . . . trying to get the client to come a bit earlier?
d. I would . . . . you to re-invest elsewhere.
e. I think . . . . send them by courier.
f. If I . . . . you, I'd try faxing them.
g. I think it's about . . . . we got a new one.
h. You . . . . ringing their accounts people. The personal touch sometimes works.

EXERCISE 2

Two business colleagues are discussing a busy schedule. Complete all the expressions used to give advice.

1. They've put back the Paris meeting to Friday morning.
2. Well, you'd . . . . fly out on Thursday evening then.
3. No, I can't do that. I've got to see a customer here on Thursday evening.
4. Why . . . . call the customer now and see if that meeting can be brought forward to today?
5. No that's impossible. I've already changed the time of the meeting once and I think he's busy today anyway.
6. In that case, you . . . . to get an early flight on Friday.
7. Yes, I . . . . I could fly out on Friday morning but the problem is that I've got another meeting back here on Friday afternoon.
8. I think you . . . . phone them now and try and put the Friday afternoon meeting back to next week.
9. That's not a bad idea. Next week would be much more convenient.

Unit 2.7   What a Mess!
Language focus – prepositions of place

Martha's office is in a terrible mess. Help her find her things. Use each of the following once:

against	*all over*	*behind*	*between*
in front of	*next to*	*from*	*on top of*
over	*through*	*under*	*out of*

1. Her bottle of water is standing . . . . the computer.
2. The mouse is hanging . . . . the lamp.
3. Her coffee mug is . . . . the pile of books.
4. Her diary is standing . . . . the computer.
5. Her sweater is hanging . . . . one of the drawers.
6. The office cat is coming in . . . . the window.
7. Her radio is . . . . the computer.
8. Her keyboard is leaning . . . . the desk.
9. Her scarf is hanging . . . . the back of her chair.
10. The company report is sandwiched . . . . two dictionaries.
11. Her floppy disks are lying . . . . the desk.
12. Her son James is sitting . . . . the desk.

Unit 2.8   The Root of the Problem
Language focus – comparing

Fit the following five sentences spoken by B into the dialogue below:

1. I agree that it was unhelpful, but we only owed a comparatively small amount of money to the banks last year and interest rates were a good deal lower than they've been for some time .
2. yes, I know , but forward investment has nothing to do with the reasons for last years problems . The oil price rise was the main reason.
3. OK . I think we'll have to agree to differ. We clearly have very different views on this.
4. Yes, I agree, but only up to a point . The falling dollar made our exports much more expensive- particularly to the US- but the main reason for our problems was the increase in oil prices That was probably much more significant than the exchange rate .
5. To a certain extent, yes but I still feel that the oil price rise was the main reason. It meant Freight costs ,for example, were much higher than the present year.

A: There were a number of reasons for the problems we experienced last year, but the most important reason was the fall in the value of the dollar.

B: . . . .

A: Possibly, but oil is priced in dollars and the price increase was virtually cancelled out by the weak dollar.

B: . . . .

A: True, but they represent a very small percentage of our total costs. Other factors were far more important. The 2% increase in interest rates had a much bigger effect than we thought at first.

B: . . . .

A: No, but the interest rate rise meant that it was more expensive for us to borrow more money for investment in new projects.

B: . . . .

A: I'm sorry. I simply can't accept that. The fact is that the weak dollar brought about most of our problems. Sales fell by 10%. That was nothing to do with oil.

B . . . .

GRAMMAR SEARCH

Underline all the expressions which compare things. Make sure you underline the whole expression, for example <u>a much bigger effect than</u>.

GRAMMAR NOTE

Notice the expression *We'll have to agree to differ*. This expression is used when it is impossible to agree on a particular point and you want to move on.

Unit 2.9   Recruiting Staff
Language focus – the most common words

All of the words in the list below are among the most common 200 words in English. Use them to complete the sentences:

little	work	make	must	same
another	each	again	without	sort
though	kind	right	place	against

1. I don't think he's the right . . . . of person for this company.
2. He has some good points, ...
3. In the first place, he has done this kind of . . . . before.
4. In fact, he did almost the . . . . job when he was in America.
5. And, don't forget he . . . . be used to the kind of market we deal with.
6. . . . . point in his favour is that he speaks several languages fluently.
7. He might be able to . . . . a useful contribution to our sales team.
8. On the other hand, ... of the other candidates has something going for him.
9. They all have the right . . . . of qualifications.
10. He is the only one . . . . direct experience of managing a sales team.
11. Having said that, he has relatively . . . . experience in managing a budget.
12. I think we will need to see each of the candidates individually . . . .
13. They all have points in their favour and points . . . .
14. The thing is, we must have the right person in . . . . very soon.
15. Let's hope we make the . . . . decision.

EXERCISE 2

Look through the examples again. Find 6 which begin with a short introductory phrase. Underline these phrases. Make sure you know the equivalent phrases in your own language.

Notice the expression *On the other hand*. We use this expression to present the opposing side of an argument, for example: *On the one hand he is very skilful and talented, but on the other (hand) he is rather unreliable.*

GRAMMAR NOTE

'Good English' does not always mean using lots of difficult words. You can improve your English a lot by learning to use the most common words in new ways. When you are reading English, always look at the words *in front of* and *following* those words you already know. This will help you to learn lots of useful multi-word expressions.

Unit 2.10   Suggesting what to do
Language focus – negative questions

A good way to present a different view in a pleasant way is to say:

NOT   June would be better.   BUT   Wouldn't June be better?
       It's too early.   Isn't it too early?

Now change these in a similar way:

1. We could wait for a few weeks.

   . . . .

2. It'd be better to decide immediately.

   . . . .

3. We could both take our cars.

   . . . .

4. We really should consult the others.

   . . . .

5. July would be too late.

   . . . .

6. We promised, so we should reply today.

   . . . .

7. It'll be quicker to e-mail them.

   . . . .

8. We've got to increase our offer.

   . . . .

9. We could share costs with them.

   . . . .

10. They are expecting an answer by 5 o'clock.

   . . . .

GRAMMAR NOTE

Notice these ways of making a difficult suggestion more tactful:

This is too late.
> *Is that too late?* (more tentative)
> *Isn't that too late?* (even more tentative)

That is too expensive.
> *That might be too expensive.*
> *I think that might be too expensive.*
> *Do you think that might be too expensive?*
> *Don't you think that might be too expensive?*

34

Unit 2.11   Being Tactful
Language focus – modals and modifiers

As we saw in Unit 2.10, often you do not want to just 'state the facts', instead you want to soften the impact of what you say by being less direct. Use the words given in brackets to change these sentences to make them less direct.

1. Your order is going to be late. *(may, slightly delayed)*

. . . .

2. We want you to reply immediately. *(would, grateful)*

. . . .

3. You've made a mistake on the invoice. *(there, seem)*

. . . .

4. You still owe us £280. *(there, seem, outstanding)*

. . . .

5. You haven't given us the discount you promised us. *(we, not seem, receive)*

. . . .

6. Our prices will go up from Jan 1st. *(we, may, slight increase)*

. . . .

7. You haven't enclosed the complete packing list as requested by us. *(seem)*

. . . .

8. The delivery will be late because of problems in our finishing shop. *(you, may, experiencing, few)*

. . . .

GRAMMAR NOTE

There are two main ways of being diplomatic in the examples above. What is important in examples 1, 6 and 8?

. . . .

. . . .

. . . .

Which word is particularly useful in the other examples?

. . . .

These seem to be slightly damaged.

Unit 2.12   Yet More Problems
Language focus – *have something done*

EXERCISE 1

Complete the responses with these words, then match the statements with the responses:

decorated   serviced   posted   drawn up   translated   installed

STATEMENTS
1. The photocopier isn't working properly.
2. This office is looking very smart.
3. I think we agree on all points. All we need now is a contract.
4. I need to have these letters typed. Could you ask someone to do them?
5. Mr Johnson still hasn't called.
6. It's very difficult to get an outside line. All the phones seem to be busy.
7. I'm afraid you won't be able to send it by fax because our machine is temporarily out of order.
8. What about this registered letter? Is anyone going to the post office?
9. I've got a problem with my car again.
10. I can't read part of this document. It seems to be in a foreign language.

RESPONSES
a. Right. I'll have one . . . . as soon as possible.
b. That's strange. We had ten new lines . . . . only last week.
c. Just leave it with me. I'll have it . . . .
d. Right. We'll have to call the service engineer.
e. You'll have to have it . . . . :
f. Really? I thought you only had it . . . . a couple of days ago.
g. Sorry. There's no-one available. You'll have to do them yourself.
h. Yes. We had it . . . . last week.
i. I see. Well, I'll have to post it to you then.
j. Really? I suppose I'll have to call him again then.

Find six examples of *to have something done*. We use this form when the subject of the sentence arranges for the action to be done by someone else.

EXERCISE 2

Rewrite the following sentences in the correct order:
1. we of made a contract the lot changes had to

. . . .
2. had first the removed penalty we clauses

. . . .
3. the then had limit time extended we

. . . .
4. option we a then added had renewal

. . . .
5. re-translated finally had the we contract whole

. . . .

Section 3
Business Travel

Unit 3.1   Talking about your Job
Language focus – question formation

EXERCISE 1

Rearrange the following to make questions you might ask someone on business.

1. here are on business you?

   . . . .

2. line business what are in you of?

   . . . .

3. do do exactly you what?

   . . . .

4. long you have doing been that how?

   . . . .

5. you did what do that before?

   . . . .

6. travelling much involve does job the?

   . . . .

7. you your do spend of whereabouts time most?

   . . . .

8. visit first London this is to your?

   . . . .

9. you arrive did when?

   . . . .

10. here for long you are how?

   . . . .

EXERCISE 2

Match the questions above with these answers:

a. A couple of days ago.
b. Oh, everywhere really, but especially the EU countries.
c. No, I've been here several times before.
d. Quite a lot – especially in Europe.
e. I work for a pharmaceuticals company.
f. Oh, for about 5 years now, I suppose.
g. I'm staying until next Friday.
h. I worked for another pharmaceuticals company in the Sales Department.
i. I'm in charge of the Sales and Marketing Department.
j. Yes, I'm here to meet some clients.

GRAMMAR NOTE

The question *Whereabouts?* often follows the question *Where are you from?* It means *Where exactly?* For example: *Where are you from?* > *I'm from Spain. Really? Whereabouts?* > *Madrid.*

Unit 3.2   Changing Plans
Language focus – present and past continuous

EXERCISE 1

The present continuous is used to talk about the future when the arrangement has already been made:

I can't make next week, I'm afraid. I'm flying to Germany on Sunday.

If these were your plans for next week, what would you answer if someone suggests a meeting on different days?

Monday:	Show Japanese visitors round the factory
Tuesday:	Prepare report for Board Meeting
Wednesday:	Board Meeting (present report)
Thursday:	Day off: play golf if weather OK
Friday:	Brief sales team

1. Monday . . . .
2. Tuesday . . . .
3. Wednesday . . . .
4. Thursday . . . .
5. Friday . . . .

EXERCISE 2

Here is your diary for the first week of March. You have had to change your plans for every single working day:

I was going to brief the Board, but now I'm meeting the French team.

Write about the other days in the same way.

Mar 6 . . . .

. . . .

Mar 7 . . . .

. . . .

Mar 8 . . . .

. . . .

Mar 9 . . . .

. . . .

Mar 10 . . . .

. . . .

MARCH

Sun 4

. . . .
Mon 5

~~Brief Board~~
Meet French team . . . .
Tue 6

~~Visit trade fair~~
Brief Board . . . .
Wed 7

~~Prepare brochure~~
Show Kenji round factory . . . .
Thu 8

~~Lunch: Anne & Peter~~
Lunch Kenji . . . .
Fri 9

~~Finish brochure~~
Inspect new factory site . . . . . .
Sat 10

~~Show Kenji round factory~~
Visit trade fair . . . .

Unit 3.3   Out and About
Language focus – fixed expressions

EXERCISE 1

Where would you hear the following? Match each of the following remarks with one of the situations below.

1. Four twenties and two tens, please.
2. I'm sorry, I'm a stranger here myself.
3. I'm sorry, I haven't got anything smaller.
4. I'm sorry, I didn't quite catch that.
5. Excuse me, I wonder if you can help me . . .
6. Is anyone sitting here?
7. Well done, please.
8. What time do you make it?
9. No thanks. I've just had one.
10. It's all right, I can manage.

SITUATIONS

a. When paying with a high-value note for something relatively inexpensive
b. When you want to sit down (on a train, for example)
c. When you are offered help but you don't need it
d. When you refuse something – a coffee, a meal, a cup of tea
e. When you can't help someone who asks you for directions in the street
f. When you need some information
g. When cashing a traveller's cheque
h. When you are asked how you would like your steak
i. When you didn't hear something clearly and want it to be repeated
j. When you want to check the time

EXERCISE 2

Rewrite the following to make things you might hear or say in a restaurant.
1. menu I the please see can?
. . . .
2. order I I'm didn't but this sorry.
. . . .
3. wine see would the you to list like?
. . . .
4. some could more have please I bread?
. . . .
5. I please have can bill the?
. . . .
6. Visa take you do?
. . . .

Unit 3.4   Rail Travel
Language focus – questions

EXERCISE 1

Rewrite the following sentences to make questions used when you are travelling:

1. to train what is next Paris time the

. . . .

2. long does to take it there how get

. . . .

3. is much return how a

. . . .

4. need I a reservation do

. . . .

5. there car train is restaurant on the a

. . . .

6. train it direct is a

. . . .

7. the I return can a for seat journey reserve

. . . .

8. can some change money I where

. . . .

9. dispenser a there cash here is near

. . . .

10. office what this time close does

. . . .

NOTE: A machine where you can get cash automatically with your card is often called a *hole-in-the-wall*; Americans usually call it an *ATM*.

EXERCISE 2

Rewrite the first six questions starting in the way indicated:

1. Can you tell me . . . .
2. Do you know . . . .
3. Can you tell me . . . .
4. Do you know . . . .
5. Can you tell me . . . .
6. Do you know . . . .

GRAMMAR NOTE

Study the difference in word order in these questions. Notice how the verb moves to the end:

 Where is the station?
 Do you know where the station is?

Unit 3.5   How to get there
Language focus – the imperative, prepositions

EXERCISE 1

Complete the instructions by filling in the missing prepositions.

EXERCISE 2

When this company has visitors coming to its office, it issues them with a set of instructions on how to get there. Put the instructions in the correct order.

How to Get to My Office

1. About half way . . . . this street . . . . the left, you'll see a large white building. This is our building.

2. Go . . . . the glass doors of the main entrance. Just . . . . the doors there's a lift. Take the lift and go up . . . . the reception desk . . . . the 6th floor.

3. Once you've signed in, go down the corridor past reception and go up the stairs . . . . the end of the corridor.

4. When you get out of the lift, you'll see a reception desk . . . . your right.

5. On the other side of the bridge, you'll come to a crossroads.

6. My office is the third on the left, opposite the entrance . . . . the cafeteria.

7. At the top turn left and go . . . . the door marked 'Sales Department'.

8. Go . . . . across and then take the first road on the left. This is Acacia Avenue.

9. You can get a taxi if you like but it's probably easier to walk. When you come out of the tube station, turn left and walk . . . . the bridge.

10. You'll probably have to show some ID . . . . the desk and they'll give you a security pass.

9										

Unit 3.6   Air Travel
Language focus – adverbs

First decide where the words given fit into the sentences. Then rearrange the sentences in each paragraph so that they make a complete text.

Paragraph 1   *even*   *never*   *usually*

1. Indeed, many of them fly club class on very short routes within Europe.
2. And surveys have also shown that many fly economy class on business.
3. Most businessmen prefer to fly first or club class.

Correct order: . . . .

Paragraph 2   *always*   *also*   *often*   *now*

1. For example, some executives stay in the most expensive hotels.
2. They are trying other ways of saving money.
3. Whilst there, they run up large bills entertaining clients.
4. However, some companies are encouraging their employees to fly economy class.

Correct order: . . . .

Paragraph 3   *frequently*   *currently*   *rarely*

1. And executives believe that such an attitude to expenses indicates a lack of confidence on the part of senior management.
2. Despite the negative reaction of their employees, many companies are introducing economy drives.
3. Such economy drives succeed, however, without the co-operation of employees.

Correct order: . . . .

GRAMMAR NOTE

Adverbs of frequency – *sometimes, never, usually* and *often* – go between the subject and the verb, for example: *She **often** travels by train.*
If there is an auxiliary verb, the adverb goes between the auxiliary verb and the main verb, for example: *He has **never** been to the USA.*

Unit 3.7   At a Trade Fair
Language focus – first conditionals

In the following conditional sentences, match the beginnings and the endings:

1. If you need to speak to me next week . . .
2. If you don't mind waiting for a few minutes . . .
3. If you would like a copy of next year's brochure . . .
4. If you let me have your card . . .
5. If you order a box today . . .
6. If you let me know exactly what you want . . .
7. If you come back at 3 o'clock . . .
8. If you leave me details of the services you are offering . . .
9. If you require a demonstration of any of the products in our brochure . . .

a. . . . I'll send you one as soon as it's ready.
b. . . . I'll send you an information pack.
c. . . . we can design something that meets your specific requirements.
d. . . . I'll get back to you if we're interested.
e. . . . my colleague will be happy to speak to you as soon as he's free.
f. . . . I'll introduce you to our Sales Manager. He should be back by then.
g. . . . please give me a ring. Here's my business card.
h. . . . please let me know which ones you are interested in and I will arrange it.
i. . . . we will be able to offer you a special discount.

Go back and underline the <u>whole</u> verb in each part of all the sentences, for example *don't mind waiting, should be back.*

GRAMMAR NOTE

The word *will* does not usually occur in the *if* part of the sentence.

You may find *would* in the *if* part of the sentence in the expression *would like*, for example: *If you would like more copies, please let us know.*

In the main clause you often find the following:

will, 'll	*If you get the tickets, I'll give you a lift.*
the imperative	*If you're passing the station, get me a timetable.*
the present simple	*If it's wet, I take the car.*
a modal	*If you're early, you must drop in for a chat.*

Section 4
Facts and Figures

Unit 4.1 Talking Figures
Language focus – numbers

EXERCISE 1

There is a mistake in each of the following expressions involving numbers. Find it, and correct it.

1. three hours and a half
2. one thousand and two hundred and twenty-two
3. seven past four
4. flight number – BA eight hundred fifty eight
5. five o'clock pm
6. the room is three metres times four metres
7. three hundreds of people
8. four point five hundred and sixty-nine
9. two and a half pounds (£2.50)

EXERCISE 2

Express the following numbers in words:

1. 1½ h (two ways)

. . . .

2. 2.075

. . . .

3. 00 – 44 – 1424 – 223344

. . . .

4. 11.50am (two ways)

. . . .

5. 33.3%

. . . .

6. 125

. . . .

7. BA 856

. . . .

8. 12.11.1995 (two ways – GB and US)

. . . .

9. 2001

. . . .

10. 100 kph

. . . .

Unit 4.2   Symbols
Language focus – numbers and symbols

EXERCISE 1

Write these e-mail addresses and websites in words

1. malpress@aol.com

. . . .

2. http/www. commcol.co.uk

. . . .

Notice how to say these symbols:

@ = at   . = dot   / = slash

Write two electronic addresses you need to give or use. Write them in the usual way, then in words as you would say them when you are giving someone the information.

. . . .

. . . .

EXERCISE 2

Write these in full in words, including all the numbers and symbols.

1. Credit note No. 75/12C

. . . .

2. The rate is £62/person/day, including VAT.

. . . .

3. Items marked * carry a 20% discount.

. . . .

4. £1 = $1.65 approx.

. . . .

5. Turnover is now £6.5m pa.

. . . .

6. The room is about 3m x 4m.

. . . .

7. My account number is 32-26-42.

. . . .

8. It was only 18°C yesterday.

. . . .

NOTE

We usually say *a*, not *one*. Use *one* (strong stress) to correct a mistake:
    An orange juice, two beers and a glass of white wine.
    >Certainly – an orange juice, a beer and two glasses of white wine.
    *No, **one** white wine, and **two** beers.*

Unit 4.3   Change and Development
Language focus – past simple and present perfect

Look at the following graph.

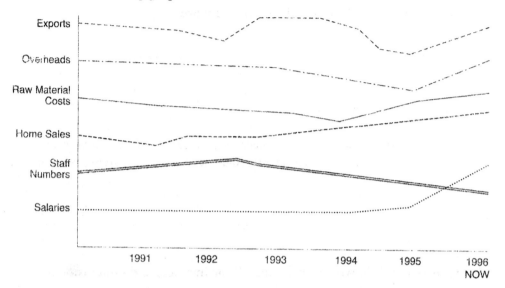

Now use the information shown to complete the following sentences using an appropriate form of the verb given. There may be more than one possible answer in some cases. Check in the key.

1. Exports . . . . significantly between 1991 and 1992.   *(fall)*
2. Since 1995 they . . . . steadily, however.   *(rise)*
3. Overheads . . . . sharply since last year.   *(rise)*
4. There . . . . a gradual fall in the price of raw materials between 1993 and 1995, but the price . . . . considerably in 1996. *(be, rise)*
5. Domestic sales . . . . steadily over the past 4 years.   *(increase)*
6. The workforce . . . . by 25% since 1994.   *(shrink)*
7. The workforce . . . . by 10% between 1991 and 1992.   *(grow)*
8. Salary costs . . . . sharply over the last few years.   *(go up)*
9. Overheads . . . . slightly in 1993.   *(fall)*
10. There . . . . a slight fall in domestic sales in 1991.   *(be)*

GRAMMAR NOTE

We usually use the past simple to describe completed events or actions in the past – *Prices **went up** in 1995. Salary costs **increased** between 1994 and 1996.*
If there is also a present time reference which relates the present to a past event then we use the present perfect form – *Prices **have increased** steadily over the past 4 years.* To emphasise the process over the whole period we use the present perfect continuous – *Prices **have been increasing** steadily over the past 4 years.*

Unit 4.4   Reporting Changes
Language focus – past simple and present perfect

Complete the voice balloons using the following:

a. *went down slightly*
b. *have gone up considerably*
c. *have levelled off*
d. *rose slightly*
e. *fell quite sharply*

f. *fluctuated*
g. *increased dramatically*
h. *remained steady*
i. *have remained constant*

1. . . . .

2. . . . .

3. . . . .

4. . . . .

5. . . . .

6. . . . .

7. . . . .

8. . . . .

9. . . . .

Unit 4.5   Looking at the Figures
Language focus – comparatives

EXERCISE 1

Rewrite these expressions of comparison in the correct order:

1. twice much as as
....
2. as as almost much
....
3. than bigger far
....
4. slightly than cheaper
....
5. more much than expensive
....
6. expensive than much less
....
7. as than as more twice expensive
....
8. as as not nearly much
....

EXERCISE 2

Now look at the chart below:

Raw materials expenditure	£15m	Labour costs	£16m
Advertising expenditure	£4m	Marketing	£2m
Research	£1.4m	Overheads	£26m
Sales in Europe	£20	US sales	£6m
Operating costs	£10m	Transportation	£3m
Domestic labour	£16 per hour	Overseas labour	£7ph
Air travel to Paris	£130	Rail travel	£ 135

Compare the following costs using each of the expressions from Exercise 1 once.

1. Raw materials and labour costs.

The amount spent on raw materials is almost as much as the amount spent on labour.
....

2. Advertising and marketing.

....

3. Raw materials and overheads.

....

4. Sales in Europe and sales in the USA.

....

5. Operating costs and transportation costs.

....

6. Transportation costs and operating costs.

....

7. The hourly domestic labour rate and the hourly overseas labour rate.

....

8. The cost of a plane ticket to Paris and the cost of a rail ticket.

....

Unit 4.6   Forecasting
Language focus – future expressions

Complete the voice balloons using the following:

a. *is expected to rise slowly*
b. *going to peak*
c. *may fall suddenly*
d. *should fall steadily*
e. *to stabilise*

f. *going to bottom out*
g. *likely to double*
h. *probably going to halve*
i. *to decrease rapidly*

1. . . . .   2. . . . .   3. . . . .

4. . . . .   5. . . . .   6. . . . .

7. . . . . , ...   8. . . . .   9. . . . .

51

Unit 4.7 Rough Figures
Language focus – approximating

Match each of the following expressions with one of the pictures:

a. *Come back about two-ish.*

b. *It should take about 15 minutes or so.*

c. *We'll meet round about the 15th.*

d. *He's about sixty.*

e. *She's thirtyish.*

f. *It's about 20 miles from here.*

g. *I'll call again in about half an hour.*

h. *Business picked up in the mid-eighties.*

i. *It costs about $50.*

j. *It must be about minus 10 this morning.*

k. *We could offer a discount of about 5%, I suppose.*

l. *Prices are about 4 times higher than they were 10 years ago.*

m. *There must be about a dozen.*

n. *It takes 10 minutes or so to get there.*

1. . . . .

2. . . . .

3. . . . .

4. . . . .

5. . . . . 6. . . . .

7. . . . . 8. . . . .

9. . . . . 10. . . . .

11. . . . . 12. . . . .

13. . . . . 14. . . . .

Unit 4.8   Room for Manoeuvre
Language focus – being deliberately imprecise

Often in business we do not want to give an exact answer. Lots of expressions help us to give numbers, dates, quantities etc, so that we have room for manoeuvre and the chance to change them a little later in the discussion.

EXERCISE 1

Complete the following expressions with one of these. Use each expression once:

around	between	towards	give or take
less	roughly	region	not more than

a. somewhere in the . . . . of 200 to 250
b. somewhere . . . . ten and twelve thousand
c. sometime . . . . the middle of September
d. about £5000, ... a couple of hundred either way
e. . . . . 7%, perhaps a bit more
f. not . . . . than £10000
g. . . . . the end of the year
h. . . . . five or six

EXERCISE 2

Use each of the expressions to complete one of these:

1. What sort of return can we expect?
   > . . . . , but I doubt it.
2. How many more weeks before you can say for certain – nine, ten?
   > No, no, ... at the most. I doubt if it will take as long as that.
3. When do you think everything will be in place?
   > . . . . but don't hold me to that; all sorts of things could go wrong.
4. Do you think £5000 will cover it?
   > Certainly not. We're looking at . . . . , maybe even a bit more than that.
5. How much will a new one cost?
   > . . . . Different models don't vary by much these days.
6. What sort of salary do you think we'll have to offer?
   > . . . . You can't really offer less than 10K these days.
7. Can you give me a ballpark figure for the number of units you might need?
   > . . . . maybe more. It's difficult to say until we have more details.
8. When will it be ready?
   > . . . . , I hope – mid-January at the latest.

Look back at the answers and underline all the expressions the speaker uses to make the answer a bit less precise, and so leave room for small changes later, for example, *I doubt it*.

Section 5
Presentations

Unit 5.1   Describing a Process
Language focus – present simple active and passive

EXERCISE 1

The following are the different stages involved in sending a message by e-mail.
Complete each sentence by using one of these verbs:

use	*write*	*address*	*convert*
read	*check*	*travel*	*turn*

1. First the sender . . . . the message on her wordprocessor.
2. She . . . . it to the receiver's e-mail number.
3. The sender's modem . . . . the message into an electronic signal.
4. Messages . . . . from sender to recipient along conventional
   telephone lines.
5. Some international messages . . . . a satellite link.
6. The recipient's modem . . . . the signal into a language that can
   be . . . . by the recipient's computer software.
7. When the recipient . . . . the e-mail box, he can see that a message
   has arrived.
8. Finally, he opens the e-mail box, ... the message and, if necessary,
   replies using the same procedure.

GRAMMAR NOTE

Notice how the general description of a process is given using the present simple.

EXERCISE 2

Look at the sentences about e-mail below and put the words in the correct order.
In each case, you need to use the passive.

1. messages quickly is to send e-mail and efficiently used

   . . . .

2. via messages sent modem are a

   . . . .

3. anyone messages be system sent to compatible with a can

   . . . .

4. multi-national is e-mail used by often companies

   . . . .

5. this saved of time is in lot way a

   . . . .

6. improved e-mail communication by efficiency been has introducing for

   . . . .

56

Unit 5.2   Describing a Product
Language focus – present simple active and passive

EXERCISE 1

Complete the sentences below using the following verbs in the passive:

take	make up	transmit	make	process
store	use	display	operate	power

1. This machine . . . . of four basic parts.
2. The frame . . . . of lightweight plastic.
3. The machine . . . . by a small electric motor.
4. It . . . . by pressing this small orange button.
5. The machine . . . . for measuring levels of static electricity.
6. Readings . . . . by a small electronic sensor.
7. The information . . . . to the machine's inbuilt computer.
8. The information . . . . by the computer.
9. The readings . . . . on the visual display unit.
10. Previous readings . . . . in the computer's memory.

EXERCISE 2

What everyday things are being described in the following?

1. It consists of two moving parts and is made of metal or plastic. It is used for cutting, especially paper.
2. They are made of thin, clear plastic and are sold in boxes of 100. They are very useful if you are giving a presentation.
3. They are usually made of metal or plastic-coated metal and are used to keep pieces of paper together.
4. These are by far the most convenient way to pay hotel and restaurant bills, particularly while travelling abroad.
5. The minibar is no use if you haven't got one of these metal things. An essential tool for the traveller.
6. People use them everywhere and annoy everyone else. One of the few things where people boast, "*Mine is smaller than yours*".

GRAMMAR NOTE

Notice when we want to describe a thing we often say:

what it is used for:	*it is used for cutting*
what it is made of:	*made of thin, clear plastic.*

Unit 5.3   Describing Current Trends
Language focus – the present continuous

EXERCISE 1

Rearrange these words to form sentences:

1. targeting a Europe lot companies are now Eastern of
   A . . . .
2. European some Eastern growing quickly economies are very
   Some . . . .
3. these companies foreign are in numerous countries investing
   Numerous . . . .
4. to companies are joint trying ventures many establish
   Many . . . .
5. in some European now currencies rising value Eastern are
   Some . . . .
6. under goods companies are these producing licence in countries some
   Some . . . .
7. is the of goods improving quality domestic
   The . . . .
8. improving the other of and services is also quality hotels
   The . . . .
9. output rising industrial again is
   Industrial . . . .
10. is unemployment unfortunately the rising also rate
    Unfortunately, ...

EXERCISE 2

Find eight important word partnerships in the above:

	share	>	market share

1. . . . . joint ventures	5. . . . . under licence
2. . . . . goods	6. . . . . in value
3. economies	7. . . . . is improving
4. . . . . rate	8. industrial . . . .

GRAMMAR NOTE

We often use the present continuous to describe the **current** situation: *The pound is falling against the dollar.* Often it contrasts with the present simple for the **general** situation: *Unemployment usually rises in the winter months, but it is falling at the moment.*

Unit 5.4   Presenting an Argument
Language focus – sequencers

Rearrange these sentences to make a complete summary:

1. As far as cost is concerned, this option is clearly the best. It is much cheaper to implement than the others and the financial risks are negligible.
2. Moving on to human resources, I feel that this is the option that will be most acceptable to our workforce. There are several reasons for this. First and foremost, this option will not involve any redundancies.
3. There are a number of reasons for choosing Option A. First and foremost, it is the most attractive option.
4. In short, it is exactly what this company needs.
5. Finally, there is the question of planning and the future direction of this company.
6. By 'attractive' I mean that it is the option which is the best for our company in all the areas of greatest concern.
7. In addition, it can be implemented almost immediately, and there will be no need to obtain extra funding from the banks, which would be the case with the other options.
8. I believe that Option A is the one which is most in tune with both our short-term and long-term plans. It is modern, progressive and has great potential.
9. In particular I suggest that there are three main areas to consider: cost, human resources and future planning.
10. Secondly, a staff retraining programme will not be necessary and, thirdly, we will be able to implement this option without introducing shift work.

Write your answers here:

3									

Go back and underline all the expressions used to connect ideas, for example: *Moving on . . .*

GRAMMAR NOTE

The expression *As far as X is/are concerned . . .* can be used to introduce a different topic. For example: *As far as sales are concerned, business is good at the moment.* It can also be used to refer to your own opinion, as in *As far as I am concerned, I think we should go ahead.*

Unit 5.5   Launching a New Project
Language focus – adverbial linking phrases

The following is an extract from a presentation given by the Marketing Director of a company launching a new product. Complete the extract using the following words and expressions:

furthermore	*however*	*as far as ... is concerned*
last but not least	*to begin with*	*for example*
apart from this	*on the other hand*	*I'd like to start*

1. . . . . by outlining some of the advantages of our new product.
2. . . . . , it is the most advanced product of its type currently on the market.
3. . . . . , it is equipped with a number of features that are not to be found in similar devices produced by our competitors.
4. . . . . , it is guaranteed 100% waterproof.
5. Equivalent products produced by our competitors, ... , are water-resistant, not water-proof.
6. . . . . obvious advantage, it is also shock-resistant and dust-proof.
7. . . . . price . . . . , I am sure that our product is the most competitive on the market.
8. It is not only price that makes this product attractive, ...
It is also guaranteed for no less than 20 years.
9. . . . . , we can offer retailers a substantial discount on bulk orders purchased direct from the factory.

GRAMMAR NOTE

When beginning a presentation, we often use the expressions *I'd like to start/begin by* . . . + the *-ing* form of the verb. Similarly, when ending a presentation, we use *I'd like to conclude/end by* + the *-ing* form of the verb.

Unit 5.6   Market Study
Language focus – adverbial expressions

The following is an extract from a presentation given by the Sales Director of a UK company that sells widely in Europe. Complete the text using the following pairs of words or phrases:

a. to be frank + tell
b. remain + however
c. re-think + accordingly
d. to give just one example + break into
e. target + in particular

f. first of all + feel
g. similarly + seem
h. continue + poor
i. in addition + mention
j. incidentally + believe

AN OVERVIEW OF THE MARKET

1. We intend to . . . . the European market and . . . . the German market.
2. We will therefore need to . . . . our marketing strategy . . . .
3. . . . . , I should also . . . . the fact that sales in other European countries have been extremely sluggish recently.
4. Sales in the Mediterranean countries in particular . . . . to be . . . .
5. We hope that sales in France will . . . . fairly stable, ...
6. . . . . , I also . . . . that some of the current problems have been caused by weaknesses in our management structure.
7. . . . . , I . . . . that certain people have not been pulling their weight.
8. And, ... , I have to . . . . you that a number of basic mistakes have been made.
9. . . . . , the opportunity to . . . . the developing markets in Eastern Europe was missed.
10. . . . . , we . . . . to have failed to take advantage of the export opportunities provided by the weakness of the pound sterling.

GRAMMAR NOTE

Other expressions can be used to replace certain of the above. For example:
> similarly / likewise
> to be frank / frankly
> to give just one example / for example / for instance
> first of all / in the first place

Unit 5.7   Sales Presentation
Language focus – comparatives

Fill the gaps in the following presentation with these expressions:

a. *there is no comparison*	g. *much better*
b. *much wider*	h. *considerably lower*
c. *more reliable than*	i. *in comparison with*
d. *much more up-market*	j. *slightly more economical than*
e. *more efficient*	k. *a lot faster than*
f. *slightly less expensive than*	l. *more solidly built*

If we compare these two models, you can see immediately that Car X has considerable advantages (1) . . . . Car Y. First of all, there is the question of price. At £18,000, Car X is (2) . . . . Car Y, which costs £18,250. Secondly, there is the question of fuel economy. On average, Car X will do 20 kilometres per litre and this makes it (3) . . . . Car Y, which averages 19.2 kpl. Then we come to the question of speed. X has a top speed of 190 kph and this is (4) . . . . Y, which can only reach 150 kph.

As far as maintenance is concerned, (5) . . . . – with Car X we offer a 2-year guarantee for all parts and labour and this represents a (6) . . . . deal than Car Y, where there is only a 6-month guarantee. In addition, with X we can also provide a (7) . . . . service network than the competition. Another factor to consider is that of reliability. Tests have shown that Car X is (8) . . . . Car Y in every respect. The engine is (9) . . . . , the bodywork is (10) . . . . and the running costs are (11) . . . . Finally, there is the question of image. Here there is no doubt that Car X has a (12) . . . . image than Car Y, as is confirmed by all our market research.

Look through and underline all the phrases which introduce a new point, for example *As far as ... is concerned.*

GRAMMAR NOTE

Short adjectives form their comparatives by adding *-er: low – lower, fast – faster.*
Longer adjectives use *more: more efficient, more expensive.*
Notice the longer phrases used to compare: *slightly / much more . . .*

Unit 5.8   Corporate Strategy
Language focus – expressions with *have*

EXERCISE 1

There are 14 examples of *have* or *had* in the text below. Mark each of them a, b, c, or d in order to match with one of the following uses:

a.   Used with *to* + infinitive to express obligation
b.   As an auxiliary verb to form the present perfect or past perfect
c.   To express possession
d   In a phrase with a noun, for example *have a meeting*

Our campany was founded in 1958. In the early years it was small and employed just 40 people. In recent years we have expanded rapidly and now the company has three separate divisions. Growth has been very steady since the mid-seventies and we managed to maintain our position during the recession of the early nineties. Last year we had some difficulty in meeting our sales targets, however, and recently we had to close one of our branches. This was an extremely difficult decistion and before we took this action, we had a series of meetings with the workforce. The meetings took place over several weeks as a large number of issues had to be discussed. We were extremely reluctant to make anyone redundant as it was the first time we had ever closed a branch. Fortunately, we have managed to find alternative positions for the majority of the staff working at the closed branch and the rest have decided to take early retirement. Now we have to consolidate our postion. We still have a large share of the domestic market and domestic sales, in general, are very good. Now we have to turn our attention to overseas markets and the main question before us today is whether we will have any problems in increasing our export sales.

EXERCISE 2

Now insert these expressions containing *have* into the gaps in the sentences. Note that you may need to change the form of the verb in some cases.

    a. have a guess   *c. have a word*   *e. have a look*
    b. have a go   *d. have a chance* *f. have no alternative*

1. There's not much we can do. We . . . . but to accept their terms.
2. Things look quite hopeful. I think we still . . . . of getting the order.
3. I'm not sure what the price is. I'll have to . . . . at the price list.
4. You seem to be having trouble with that. Why don't you let me . . . . ?
5. I didn't know the exact number, but I . . . . and, amazingly, I was absolutely right.
6. Can I . . . . with you about this fax I've just received?

63

Unit 5.9   Interrupting the Presenter
Language focus – question formation

EXERCISE 1

Match these statements or questions with the follow-up questions below. Then underline the words in the follow-up question which direct attention, for example: *more details, exactly.*

1. I have a question. Your sales figures for last year show a 15% increase in sales to the Far East.
2. I'm sorry. I'd like to go back to something you said earlier. You mentioned the possibility of an optional extension to the contract.
3. If I could just ask a question about dates.
4. When you were talking about sales targets for next year, you mentioned the possibility of offering a discount on certain products.
5. Can I ask a question at this point? I'm not entirely clear about the section of the contract that refers to maintenance.
6. Can I just stop you there for a moment? You were talking about the sales potential of this product.

a. Could you give <u>more details</u> of the procedures involved and when the guarantee on components expires?
b. When <u>exactly</u> do you expect to begin supplying the product and when do you expect delivery to be complete?
c. Could I just ask you to explain exactly how it differs from similar products produced by your competitors and what advantages there are for us in promoting your product?
d. Could you tell us exactly what you have in mind? Would this be under the same terms as the existing contract or would the terms be reviewed first?
e. Could you be more specific about this and say exactly where this increase was achieved and which products were involved?
f. Could you just clarify the details of which products you have in mind and also what sort of discounts you have in mind?

1	2	3	4	5	6

EXERCISE 2

Complete the word partnerships with words from Exercise 1.

1. . . . . the possibility
2. . . . . a discount
3. . . . . expires
4. . . . . delivery
5. . . . . a similar product
6. . . . . the same terms
7. . . . . an increase
8. . . . . details

64

Section 6
Phone and Fax

Unit 6.1   Getting Through
Language focus – *could* and *'ll*

EXERCISE 1

Complete the sentences below using the following words:

catch   called   try   again   please   someone   message   line   back   speak

1. Could I speak to . . . . in the Marketing Department, please?
2. Could you ask Mr Green to call me . . . . ?
3. Could I speak to Alan Green, ... ?
4. Could I leave a . . . . for Suzanne Butler?
5. Could you tell him I . . . . ?
6. Could you tell her I'll call . . . . tomorrow?
7. Could you hold the . . . . , please?
8. Could you . . . . again. I'm afraid it's a rather bad line.
9. Could you . . . . up? It's a terrible line and I can hardly hear you.
10. Could you repeat the date please? I didn't quite . . . . it.

EXERCISE 2

Complete these responses, then match them to the questions above:

see   soon   like   wait   hear   'll   anyone   get   back   course

a. Yes, I'll tell him as . . . . as he gets back.
b. Just a moment, I'll . . . . if he's in his office.
c. Yes, of course. I'll . . . . him to call you as soon as he gets back.
d. Yes, of . . . . It's Tuesday, July 4th.
e. Certainly. I'll see if there's . . . . there.
f. Yes, I . . . . tell her.
g. Is that better? Can you . . . . me now?
h. OK. I'll call . . . .
i. Yes, no problem. I'll . . . .
j. Yes, of course. What would you . . . . me to tell her?

GRAMMAR SEARCH

Now highlight at least 5 expressions which you find useful in the above examples, for example: *Could I leave a message, please?*

GRAMMAR NOTE

1. *Could I / you .... ?* + the base verb are the most common ways of making polite requests when using the telephone.
2. When responding to a request we often use *'ll* + the base verb, for example:
   I'll get him to call you later.

Unit 6.2   Telephone Enquiries
Language focus – responses with 'll

Complete the following mini-dialogues using one of these words for the first line:

rather	back	written
information	moment	speak
know	afraid	answer

and one of these verbs for each response:

try	see	let
put	make	get
confirm	be	need

1. We need . . . . confirmation of your booking.

   > OK, I'll . . . . it by fax.

2. I'm sorry. She's not here at the . . . .

   > That's all right. I'll . . . . again later.

3. We need to . . . . as soon as possible.

   > I'll . . . . you know by tomorrow afternoon at the latest.

4. Could you tell him today, please? It's . . . . urgent.

   > Don't worry. I'll . . . . sure he gets the message.

5. As soon as you have the information, could you get . . . . to me?

   > Of course. I'll . . . . back to you later today.

6. Could I . . . . to Mrs Ferguson?

   > Hold the line, please. I'll . . . . if she's in her office.

7. I need some . . . . about flight times.

   > Right. I'll . . . . you through to the Travel Department.

8. I'm . . . . Jack is in a meeting at the moment.

   > Don't worry. Just tell him I'll . . . . in touch when I get back.

9. When do you think you'll have an . . . . ?

   > Not before tomorrow. I'll . . . . to clear it with my boss.

GRAMMAR NOTE

We often use the 'll form in responses such as *I'll make sure he gets the message.*
Note that in speech 'll is the normal form, not *will.*

Unit 6.3 Phoning to Check
Language focus – question formation

A customer would like to place an order and pay by credit card. What questions will you need to ask so you can complete the order form?

CREDIT CARD ORDER

Card Type: VISA   MASTERCARD   EUROCARD

Name: ....

Card No: .... Expiry Date: ....

Address of Cardholder: ....

....

Mailing Address (if different): . ...

....

Method of Delivery (please tick):

    SURFACE POST ☐   AIRMAIL ☐   SHIPPER ☐

Ref No.	Quantity	Size	Colour

Use the words given to make the questions you need to ask.

1. Can you .... (name)

2. How .... (pay)

3. What .... (type of card)

4. What .... (mailing address)

5. What .... (order)

6. What ....,.................................. (card number)

7. What .... (expiry date)

8. Is there .... (reference)

9. How .... (dispatched)

10. Could .... (telephone number)

Unit 6.4   Faxing a Message
Language focus – modals

EXERCISE 1

Here are four short faxes:

> 1. Please could you confirm that you are coming on Wednesday? We need to know urgently so that we can draw up the final agenda for the meeting.

> 3. Please note that the meeting scheduled for October 11 th has now been brought forward to October 10 th. We would be very grateful if you could confirm your attendance.

> 2. Please note that Mr Tauber will be arriving on October 11 th and not on October 10 th as previously arranged.

> 4. Just to confirm the arrangements for the 15 th. When you arrive at the office. You should go to reception and ask for Mr Takahashi.

Here are 4 responses to the above faxes. Match the responses to the faxes:

a. Thanks for your fax. We note the change of date and confirm our attendance. We look forward to seeing you on the 10th.

b. Thanks for your fax. We confirm our attendance at the meeting on Wednesday. We would be very grateful if you could let us have a copy of the agenda in advance. With thanks.

c. Thanks for your fax re the meeting with Mr Takahashi. Unfortunately you did not mention a time. Could you let us know what time we should be there?

d. Thanks for your fax. No problem with the change of date. Please let your client know that we'll be at the airport to meet him.

EXERCISE 2

Complete the following sentences using one of the following modal verbs:

would	*could*	*should*	*will*

1. We . . . . be very grateful if you could reply by return.
2. Payment . . . . be made within 14 days of receipt of this invoice.
3. . . . . you confirm that payment has already been made?
4. We . . . . arrange for payment by bank transfer as soon as we receive the goods.
5. Mr Odaka . . . . be arriving on Flight OU461 on Monday 25th.
6. All telephone orders . . . . be confirmed in writing.
7. . . . . you let us have a copy of your latest price list?
8. We . . . . appreciate an early reply.

NOTE

Notice these expressions used in brief faxes:

> *Thanks for your fax.*   *Please note ...,*   *Sorry for ...,*
> *Please advise us ...*   *Please could you confirm ... .*

69

Unit 6.5   Faxing about Orders
Language focus – adverbials

EXERCISE 1

Put the adverbials in italics into an appropriate place in each sentence:
1. We are unable to forward the goods that you ordered this week.
   unfortunately
2. We will be able to complete delivery by the end of next week.
   probably
3. We have been having some problems with our database.
   recently
4. We are reviewing our ordering procedures.
   currently
5. We noticed the error before dispatching the goods.
   fortunately
6. It was entered into the database twice.
   apparently
7. Our systems ensure we pick up errors before the goods leave the factory.
   usually
8. The goods have been dispatched to you.
   just
9. We use a security company to deliver important orders.
   frequently
10. This means that we can track them at all times.
    in general

Which adverbials usually occur in initial position and which in mid position?

EXERCISE 2

In each of these sentences the adverb is in an incorrect or unusual position. Rewrite the sentence with the adverb in the most natural position:

1. I just have received your letter.

   . . . .
2. You probably are expecting an answer soon.

   . . . .
3. I try always to answer letters promptly.

   . . . .
4. I answer enquiries by fax usually.

   . . . .
5. I send normally faxes in the evening.

   . . . .
6. Our fax machine unfortunately is out of order at the moment.

   . . . .

GRAMMAR NOTE

Adverbs which comment on the whole sentence often come at the beginning. These are among the most common: *unfortunately, apparently, luckily.*

Section 7
Reports

Unit 7.1 Chairperson's Report
Language focus – past simple, present perfect

Complete this report about the history of a company. Use one of these verbs in either the past simple or present perfect:

strengthen	represent	win	employ	work	have (x 2)
face	expand	invest	take on	move	help
change	start	result	enable	grow (x 2)	go

We (1) . . . . another excellent year. I would like to thank everyone for their hard work which (2) . . . . in bringing about this success. As you know, we (3) . . . . in 1965 as a small operation producing electrical components for the car industry. At the time we (4) . . . . just 25 people; that number (5) . . . . to the present 1,200. Our turnover was just £50,000, whereas today it (6) . . . . to £35 million.

In those early years conditions were not particularly comfortable. I (7) . . . . in a tiny office with no heating, and, of course, in those days we (8) . . . . no computers, which make life so much easier today. We were based in a run-down inner-city area.
Things (9) . . . . considerably since we (10) . . . . to our current greenfield site. The early years were particularly difficult. We (11) . . . . strong competition from more powerful competitors and on several occasions we were close to going out of business. The turning point came in 1974 when we (12) . . . . a small government contract to produce electrical components for aircraft. We (13) . . . . more staff and (14) . . . . a considerable amount of money in Research and Development and (15) . . . . from strength to strength ever since.

In recent years we (16) . . . . our product range and (17) . . . . our position in the export market. These changes (18) . . . . in the strength of our current position. The recent deregulation of the markets within the European Union (19) . . . . us to increase our exports to Europe and we are now in a position to expand our European operations still further. As far as business with the rest of the world is concerned, in the early years exports to the Far East, for example, (20) . . . . less than 1% of our output, whereas now they represent nearly 15% of our total production.

Grammar Note

For actions at a particular point in the past, use the past simple; for actions linking now and a point in the past, use the present perfect. Check the examples above, using this rule. Usually you will find a phrase such as *our present position* when the present perfect is correct.

Unit 7.2   Reporting on a Meeting
Language focus – reported speech

Fill in the gaps in the text below using the information given in this short report:

> I'm afraid there are a number of problems with this agreement. First of all, we feel that your company has not been reliable on several occasions in the past. We are Particularly unhappy about the fact that there have been a number of late deliveries and these have caused us considerable problems. Another problem is that on at least five occasions you have supplied faulty parts and we have had to return these to you. In addition, some orders have arrived either incomplete or simply incorrect. There is also the problem of discount. Originally you romised us a 10% discount on orders over £10,000 but you charged us the full amount even when the bulk order was clearly stated on the order form. I'm not very happy about the prices you charge either. Other companies are offering the same products at more competitive prices and I can see no reason why we should continue purchasing from you. We will only consider continuing to buy from you if you reduce your prices. Offer a consistent discount, preferably at a higher rate, and guarantee a better quality of service and delivery.

He said (1) . . . . a number of problems with the agreement. In particular, they felt that we (2) . . . . reliable on several occasions in the past. There (3) . . . . a number of late deliveries and he said they (4) . . . . particularly unhappy about that. He also said that we (5) . . . . faulty parts on at least five occasions and that some orders (6) . . . . either incomplete or incorrect. He also mentioned the discount problem. Apparently, we (7) . . . . them a 10% discount on orders over £10,000, but (8) . . . . them for the full amount even when the bulk discount (9) . . . . clearly stated on the order form. He was unhappy about the price too. He said that other companies (10) . . . . the same products at more competitive prices and he (11) . . . . see no reason why they should continue purchasing from us. They (12) . . . . only consider continuing to buy from us if we (13) . . . . our prices, (14) . . . . a consistent discount, preferably at a higher rate, and (15) . . . . a better quality of service and delivery.

GRAMMAR NOTE

When reporting speech, verb forms are transformed into a corresponding past form. The most common ones are: *is > was, are > were, have/has > had.* Modals change in a similar way: *can > could, will > would.*

73

Unit 7.3   Business Trip Report
Language focus – reported questions

EXERCISE 1

Look at these examples of questions and how they are reported:

What's the salary? How long are the hours? When does the job actually start?
> *She asked what the salary was, how long the hours were and when the job actually started.*

Is there any overtime? Do you need a reference?
> *She asked if there was any overtime and if we needed a reference.*

Rearrange the following to make reported questions:

1. materials they would us when the be ready asked

. . . .

2. much they asked they also cost how would

. . . .

3. manager the purchasing we our asked goods usually ship how

. . . .

4. they payment what terms the were also asked

. . . .

5. had asked last they contract when finished the

. . . .

6. contract they to when the know also start wanted would

. . . .

7. asked also if price was they fixed the

. . . .

8. renewable they the if contract was asked

. . . .

EXERCISE 2

Now report the following questions about a contract in a similar way:

1. When does the contract start?
2. How many companies are involved?
3. Is there a penalty clause?
4. How many units can you supply each month?
5. How will the goods be shipped?
6. How much discount can you offer?
7. Is the agreement flexible?
8. Can you guarantee the terms?

Unit 7.4   Sales Report

Language focus – past and present tense review

The following is a Sales Manager's report on returning from a marketing trip. Complete the sentences below using the correct form of the following verbs:

experience	suffer	produce (x 2)	run out of	sign
reflect	discuss	offer (x 2)	reduce	be
pay	accept	look at	introduce	have

1. First of all, I was able to offer them a highly competitive price, at least 5% below the current market average. Secondly, I was able to offer guarantees as regards both delivery and quality, and, finally, I . . . . . . them the possibility of a flexible deal that . . . . . . the demands of the market.

2. Another problem has been a lack of flexibility by their suppliers as regards the fluctuating market for aircraft components. Apparently, there . . . . . . times when they . . . . . . raw materials and other times when they have had a large surplus.

3. I visited ABC Ltd as part of my marketing trip to a number of European countries. ABC . . . . components for aircraft and, as such, they are particularly interested in the light-weight metal alloys we . . . .

4. This means that they . . . . . . ways of saving money and one way of doing this is clearly to . . . . . . expenditure on raw materials. The prices they . . . . . . at the moment for these materials are rather higher than are justified in the current market.

5. Needless to say, they were extremely happy with these terms and I am confident that they . . . . . . them and . . . . . . a contract within the next few weeks.

6. On arrival I . . . . . . to the Managing Director and, after a brief discussion with him, I . . . . . . a meeting with the Purchasing Manager and his senior staff. We . . . . . . the needs of their company in some detail and also looked at their present suppliers.

7. In response to all of this, I was able to . . . . . . them an improved deal in all of these areas.

8. Apart from the high prices, they are also dissatisfied with the service offered by their current suppliers. They . . . . . . a number of problems with deliveries and also with the quality of some of the materials supplied.

9. They are unhappy with their present suppliers for several reasons. First, of course, there is the question of price. The aircraft industry in general . . . . . . a downturn in business and component manufacturers are obviously badly affected by this situation.

Now rearrange the paragraphs to make a complete report.

3									

GRAMMAR SEARCH

Look back at the report and underline 10 expressions where nouns or adjectives are followed by prepositions – *expenditure on, interested in* etc.

Unit 7.5 Minutes
Language focus – the passive

EXERCISE 1

The following are extracts from the minutes of a meeting. All the missing verbs should be in the passive form:

1. The minutes, which . . . . prior to the meeting, were duly signed as an accurate record.   (circulate)
2. It . . . . by all present that Bill Wilson take the chair in the absence of the MD.   (agree)
3. It . . . . that some members of the group were dissatisfied with the format of the reports.   (report)
4. As there was an increasing level of complaints about the cleanliness of the staff restaurant, it . . . . to call the catering manager to the next meeting of the group.   (decide)
5. A new system . . . . whereby each member of the group took it in turn to chair the meeting.   (propose)
6. Agreement on the future of the RB150 project . . . . after a heated debate lasting over an hour.   (reach)
7. There have been rumours about a possible hostile takeover of the company, but this . . . . by headquarters in Zurich.   (deny)
8. Without coming to any agreement on Point 8 on the agenda, the meeting . . . . , when the fire alarm went off unexpectedly. (adjourn)

EXERCISE 2

Rewrite each sentence using the verb given in the passive:

1. Analysts think that Smiths is one of the UK's leading chains. (regard)
. . . .
2. We got the information from a reliable inside source. (obtain)
. . . .
3. We OK'd the budget at our last meeting. (clear)
. . . .
4. Everyone accepted the idea. (agree, unanimously)
. . . .

GRAMMAR NOTE

The choice between active and passive depends on what comes first in the sentence. If the subject is the most important idea, the sentence will be active – *The Volvo hit a tree.* The sentence: *The old man was killed by a speeding Volvo,* is about *The man . . .* and the passive is the natural choice.

Section 8
Meetings and Negotiations

Unit 8.1   Setting the Agenda
Language focus – gerund or infinitive

Match the beginnings of the sentences below with their endings:

1. I would like to start by . . .
2. The main purpose of this meeting is to . . .
3. The first thing we need to do is . . .
4. With regard to sales, we will also look . . .
5. Then we should . . .
6. After looking at market trends . . .
7. The financial report will be followed . . .
8. Finally, after looking at management procedures, I look forward to . . .

a. analyse market trends.
b. hearing your views on the future developments of the company.
c. to review this year's sales.
d. at the performance of individual sales personnel.
e. perhaps we could turn to financial matters.
f. set our sales targets for the rest of this year.
g. by a review of management procedures.
h. thanking you all for coming today.

GRAMMAR SEARCH

a. **Which two examples contain the infinitive used to express aim or purpose?**

. . . .

b. **Find three examples of verbs followed by a preposition and either a noun or the '-ing' form of the verb.**

. . . .

GRAMMAR NOTE

After prepositions we use either a noun or the '-ing' form of the verb. For example:

> Let me start **by introducing** . . .
> Thank you **for returning** my call . . .
> I look forward **to hearing** from you again soon.

Note that in the last example, '*to*' is a preposition and not part of the infinitive. It must, therefore, be followed by the '-ing' form of the verb.

Unit 8.2 Outlining Your Position
Language focus – prepositional expressions

EXERCISE 1

Complete these statements made by the leaders of two negotiating teams:

of benefit to	as a basis for	on this basis
limited to	in favour of	at some
the possibility of	co-operate with	at this point

I'd like to start by making our position absolutely clear. What we want is an agreement that is (1) . . . . both our parties. Our basic position is that we want to (2) . . . . your company in both production and distribution in a worldwide market. This is our starting-point and we want this point to be clearly understood and to be used (3) . . . . these negotiations. Secondly, we are (4) . . . . a licensing agreement rather than a joint venture agreement. The policy of our company has always been to seek licensing agreements and we see no reason to change our position (5) . . . . Thirdly, we firmly believe that any such agreement must be on a worldwide basis and not (6) . . . . a particular geographical area. Finally, we want an agreement that does not exclude (7) . . . . the participation of a third party (8) . . . . future stage. This is our position and we hope that we will be able to proceed (9) . . . .

EXERCISE 2

opposed to	in a position	at this stage
stand on	as far as	present circumstances
preferable to	in favour of	of benefit to

Thank you for stating the position of your company so clearly. If I may, I'd now like to respond by outlining where we (10) . . . . these issues. Our starting point is also a desire for mutual co-operation with your company in the areas of production and distribution. I think both sides can agree on this point. At present, however, we are not (11) . . . . to accept that a licensing agreement is (12) . . . . a joint venture agreement. We do not normally grant licences to produce our products and we are strongly (13) . . . . a joint venture agreement in the (14) . . . . To respond to your third point, what we are looking for (15) . . . . is a limited agreement. By limited I mean that we want to limit any agreement to the countries of the Pacific rim. We are not convinced that a worldwide agreement would be (16) . . . . us at this stage. (17) . . . . your final point is concerned, we are not (18) . . . . the involvement of a third party in this agreement and we do not see any reason for the inclusion of such a clause. This is our current position.

GRAMMAR NOTE

Notice the prepositional phrases used when stating your position:

We are *in favour of* . . .   We are *opposed to* . . .

Underline all the expressions above which contain a preposition which might be useful to you when negotiating.

Unit 8.3   Points of View
Language focus – modifying adjectives

EXERCISE 1

Match the following questions and answers:

1. What do you think of this machine?
2. What's your opinion of this procedure?
3. This is our new product range. What do you think of it?
4. What about the terms of the new contract? What do you think of them?
5. Am I right in thinking you're against signing the export deal?
6. What do you think of the overall marketing strategy?
7. Have you seen these latest sales figures?
8. Have you got any thoughts on the management reorganisation?

a. It's reasonably satisfactory, but I think we need to take steps to strengthen the export division.
b. It's very effective and it saves a lot of time.
c. I think it's absolutely excellent. There's a lot of choice and the quality seems good.
d. Yes. I think it's completely unworkable in its present form.
e. Yes. I think it's long overdue and I hope it will do something to make the company much more efficient.
f. Yes. I think they're very disappointing.
g. It's clean, efficient and extremely reliable, and it doesn't need much maintenance.
h. They seem perfectly reasonable to me.

EXERCISE 2

Look carefully at the words in front of the adjectives. Underline the phrases like:

> *reasonably* satisfactory

Which of the following adjectives can be used with *absolutely* to express a very strong or even extreme opinion?

difficult	*fantastic*	*interesting*	*fascinating*
easy	*surprised*	*furious*	*amazing*
useful	*essential*	*useless*	*exhausted*
tired	*nice*	*astonished*	*angry*

GRAMMAR NOTE

To express a qualified opinion using *quite*, we usually put a stronger stress on *quite* than on the adjective it goes with. Can you say *It was **quite** interesting* and *It was quite **interesting*** to show two different meanings?

Unit 8.4   Stating Your Case
Language focus – summarising

Complete the sentences below using the following:

way	*simply*	*short*	*words*
nutshell	*frankly*	*bluntly*	*word*

1. Sales are down, costs are rising, orders are zero. In . . . . , we ...
2. The present arrangements are not satisfactory and, in fact, they are not really working for either party. To put it another . . . . , we ...
3. The flight was late, the meeting with the clients was a disaster, and, to cap it all, I missed my flight home. To put it . . . . , it ...
4. Everyone says they are unreliable. They don't answer letters, their documentation is a mess. In a . . . . , we ...
5. She's efficient, responsible and decisive. She's always done everything we've asked her to do. In a . . . . , she's ...
6. It's got a get-out clause, a penalty clause for late delivery, and they can start supplying the goods immediately. In other . . . . , it's ...
7. He's always late and he's unreliable. He's just a troublemaker. To put it . . . . , he's ...
8. You're asking far too much money for something that, quite . . . . , is lousy. I'm sorry, if I could just rephrase that, what I mean is that it ...

Now finish the above sentences by choosing the correct endings:

a.   need a new agreement.
b.   is not a particularly good product.
c.   the best candidate for the job.
d.   not the person we need.
e.   are in serious trouble.
f.   was a complete waste of time.
g.   the best possible contract we can get.
h.   don't want them as customers.

GRAMMAR NOTE

Now underline all the expressions we use when we are repeating or summarising what we have said, for example:

    In short   *In a nutshell*

Unit 8.5   Raising Doubts
Language focus – *there is / there are*

EXERCISE 1

There is used with different verb forms in many expressions to talk about problems. Arrange these words in the correct order to state problems of different kinds.

1. There can much do about it we isn't

. . . .

2. There's alternative no

. . . .

3. There's to programme been change the a

. . . .

4. There left were seats no

. . . .

5. There room not everybody for been have might

. . . .

6. There time finish yesterday enough to wasn't

. . . .

7. There's way be there time on no we'll

. . . .

8. There trouble find be when out they what's happened 'll

. . . .

EXERCISE 2

Use each of the expressions above to respond in these situations:

a.   Did you book us on the 7.30 flight?
b.   Why do you need to make an announcement?
c.   Why are we moving to a different room?
d.   Why are you still working on that today?
e.   Are you going to give them their money back?
f.   You don't seem very worried about the situation.
g.   Why do you look so worried?
h.   Why are you ringing them? It's only ten to.

EXERCISE 3

Rearrange these to make questions which contain *there*. Can you think of a situation in which you might use each one?

1.   other to there consider any are points?
2.   calls me been have for there any?
3.   else we there need talk to about is anything?
4.   finance any there be problem with will?

Unit 8.6   Decision Making
Language focus – agreeing and disagreeing

Match the following statements with the responses below:

1. I think it's a wonderful deal.
2. What we need to do is invest in the domestic market.
3. We need to borrow at least £20 million.
4. This new model is a real breakthrough.
5. The marketing strategy is very fully developed.
6. I think we should sell our Central London office. The rent is far too high.
7. It would be better to move to a greenfield site.
8. We need to put money into our current products.
9. We could consider a takeover.
10. The simplest answer is probably a joint venture agreement.

a. I agree with you up to a point but I think that's too much.
b. Sorry, I think we need something new.
c. No, I can't agree with you, I'm afraid. I think it'd be better to keep it.
d. Co-operation is the best solution, you're right there.
e. Excellent – our best deal for ages.
f. I'm afraid I think expanding exports would be better.
g. I'm in complete agreement. We need to relocate.
h. No, that's out of the question, I'm afraid. The share price is far too high.
i. It's a very clear plan. I agree entirely.
j. Yes, I'm in total agreement with you there. It's a real innovation.

GRAMMAR SEARCH

Sometimes we agree by saying so directly:

I couldn't agree more.   *I agree up to a point.*

but we also agree by using a different expression with the same meaning, or disagree by offering an alternative.

We need to put money into our current products.
> Sorry, I think we need something new.

It's a wonderful deal.
> Excellent – our best deal for ages.

Underline all the different ways of agreeing and disagreeing in the examples.

Unit 8.7   Considering Proposals
Language focus – eliminating options

EXERCISE 1

The following are part of a business meeting where an important financial decision is made. Complete them using the correct form of these verbs:

seem	examine	bring	reject	choose
put	exclude	reach	satisfy	give

1. I don't think that this will be particularly difficult because at least two of the five do not . . . . the basic criteria for the contract.

2. So, are we all agreed that we are . . . . proposals A and E?

3. I personally feel that all of these are sound proposals but that of the three, proposal C is the one we should . . . .

4. All in all, then, I strongly believe that we should opt for C and I would, therefore, like to . . . . that to the vote.

5. So, we have now had a chance to . . . . all the proposals in detail and it is now time to come to a decision.

6. It is also the most detailed, which means we can . . . . a number of other decisions today, if we choose C.

7. Right. That . . . . us to proposals B, C and D.

8. Our first task is to . . . . any which are definitely not acceptable.

9. I say this for several reasons, but mainly because C is the one which . . . . to provide the most flexibility in terms of both time and funding.

10. I'm thinking here of proposals A and E, neither of which . . . . an unconditional guarantee on the completion date.

EXERCISE 2

Now rearrange the sentences in the correct order. The first one has been done for you:

5									

GRAMMAR NOTE

Notice the expression *All in all . . . .* . This is often used to express a conclusion after several points for and against have been discussed:

   All in all, I think we should opt for A.

Unit 8.8   Emphasising a Point
Language focus – *need, must, have to*

EXERCISE 1

Complete the sentences below using the following words and phrases:

a. essential	e. straight to the point
b. over-emphasise	f. emphasise
c. more than anything else	g. important
d. crux of the matter	h. no doubt whatsoever

1. What I'd like to stress is, and I can't . . . . this enough, that sales have to improve and they have to improve now.
2. I firmly believe that what you need . . . . is a complete reorganisation of your sales department.
3. It is absolutely . . . . to have an effective sales team. And salespeople must have had effective training.
4. The . . . . is that you simply aren't aggressive enough in your approach to selling. To sell you have to push and push hard.
5. I really must stress that the most . . . . thing at this stage is not the advertising campaign but the way that we train our salespeople.
6. Advertising is one thing, but there is . . . . that having good people on the ground is the key to increased sales. You must have good people, who are trained and motivated.
7. Let me get . . . . We need action and we need it now.
8. It's impossible to . . . . the importance of the role played by the sales team, and to get the best out of them they need incentives. A bonus scheme is not essential, but it must help.

EXERCISE 2

Find 6 expressions above used to introduce and emphasise the speaker's comments.

1. *What I'd like to stress is* . . .
2. . . . .
3. . . . .
4. . . . .
5. . . . .
6. . . . .

GRAMMAR NOTE

(Have) to usually states what is necessary because of law, rules etc. *Must* is often what the speaker thinks is necessary. Does that fit the examples above? Notice in number 1 that the speaker gives the idea of real necessity by using *have to*.

Unit 8.9 Standing Your Ground
Language focus – verb + noun partnerships

EXERCISE 1

Complete the sentences below using the following words:

up to a point	*limit*	*unacceptable*	*final*	*bottom*
moving	*clear*	*unable*	*leave*	*position*

1. We've considered your offer very carefully, but I'm afraid we're
   . . . . to accept it. We're sticking to our original position.
2. I'm very sorry. This is really the . . . . line. This is the cheapest
   offer I can make and I simply can't go any lower.
3. I'm afraid that we are not able to meet the conditions that you have just
   outlined. We are prepared to be flexible . . . . but we really
   cannot accept those conditions.
4. I'm sorry but we can't accept that. Our . . . . is clear and we have
   explained it to you several times before. If you want these negotiations to
   continue, then there will have to be some concessions on your part.
5. We have made all the concessions we can make in this matter and we can
   go no further. This is our . . . . offer.
6. I'm sorry, but we're not . . . . on this one. We have already
   offered you the cheapest deal possible and it's impossible, I repeat
   impossible, for us to offer you any more discount.
7. We have made our position . . . . to you on several occasions.
   We are not prepared to accept a lower price. I'm very sorry but that's the
   way it is.
8. I'm sorry, but this is really very simple. The time clause is . . . . to
   us and we are not prepared to change our position on this.
9. Look, we can go this far but we can't go any further. We have already
   made several concessions, but we have now reached the . . . .
10. I'm sorry, but this is our position. As far as I am concerned, this is non-
    negotiable. Take it or . . . . it.

EXERCISE 2

Complete the following verb + noun expressions from the sentences above.

1. make an	4. . . . . . . concessions	7. accept a . . . . . .
2. . . . . . . the conditions	5. . . . . . . your position	8. continue . . . . . .
3. offer a	6. . . . . . . a discount	9. consider an . . . . . .

GRAMMAR SEARCH

Now find and underline 8 useful expressions to show you will not change your
position, for example: *Take it or leave it.*

Unit 8.10   Decisions and Explanations
Language focus – prepositional phrases

EXERCISE 1

First complete the explanations by filling in the missing prepositions.

EXERCISE 2

Now match the decisions with the explanations.

DECISIONS

1. After due consideration, we have decided to give the job to Ms Brookside.
2. We have finally decided to locate the new factory in Southampton.
3. We regret that we have no option but to close our office in Brussels.
4. We have reluctantly decided to dispense with the position of Marketing Director, Northern Europe.
5. Unfortunately, we have had to take the decision to terminate our contract with you.
6. Some difficult decisions have had to be made and we feel that it is in our best interests to abandon the JZ research project.
7. We have decided that the best option is for our two companies to merge.
8. We are delighted to announce that the shareholders have decided to accept our offer.

EXPLANATIONS

a. This is due to the sharp downturn . . . . the market, particularly in Scandinavia, and also to the fact that a streamlining of our European operations will mean that we will need fewer people . . . . this sector.
b. They took the decision . . . . the basis of an improved offer that made our package impossible to resist. We are sure that this decision will benefit all concerned and that the new, enlarged company will go . . . . strength . . . . strength.
c. We felt that she was the most able of the candidates . . . . the short list and it is clear that she has skills . . . . precisely the areas we need.
d. Despite our long co-operation . . . . you, we have grown increasingly dissatisfied . . . . the quality of the goods you have been supplying and, as a result, we have been forced to seek an alternative supplier.
e. We took this decision because we felt that it had considerable advantages . . . . the other possible sites. . . . . the first place, it is centrally located. Secondly, transportation links are good, and, thirdly, it is the cheapest alternative.
f. The decision was taken . . . . the basis of economic factors. Rents are increasing all the time, and we recently received a demand for a 30% increase for the next 5-year lease. This is simply not justifiable . . . . financial terms.
g. We felt that it was becoming more and more expensive and it was difficult to see when we would get a return . . . . our investment. The project is still several years . . . . the development stage and we feel that it is now time to cut our losses.
h. The reason for this is that we are currently competing . . . . each other in a shrinking market. To retain our market share we need to co-operate . . . . each other and improve the quality of our products.

Unit 8.11   Customer Feedback
Language focus – complaining

EXERCISE 1

Complete the sentences below using the following words:

> satisfied   specific   frank   dissatisfied   impressed
> appalling   surprised   helpful   unreliable   happy

SALES REPRESENTATIVE

1. As I said, this is very unusual. I'll have to check this when I get back.
2. I'm sorry to hear that. Can you say why you are . . . . ?
3. I'm very surprised. Most of our customers say how . . . . they are.
4. Only 'reasonably satisfied'. It sounds as if you've had some problems. We don't get many complaints about our products.
5. One of the main reasons for my visit here today is to get some feedback so, first of all, can you tell me if you are . . . . with the products and service we provide?
6. Really? I'm very . . . . to hear that. Could you be more . . . . ?

CUSTOMER

7. Well, to start with, your back-up and maintenance is . . . .
8. To give you one example, whenever we contact you to call out a maintenance engineer, we find the staff very unhelpful.
9. I think you should, because we are very . . . . with most other things but we have had problems with maintenance visits.
10. No, I believe you. Our problem is with the quality of your service and, to be absolutely . . . . , we are not . . . . with it.
11. That's not our experience. It's very difficult to fix an appointment, and the engineers are often extremely . . . . They simply don't turn up and we have to go through the whole process again.
12. Reasonably satisfied, I suppose.

EXERCISE 2

Now rearrange the sentences above to make a complete dialogue between the Sales Representative and the Customer.

5											

GRAMMAR NOTE

Notice the question *Could you be a bit more specific?* We say this in order to get more information. Other similar expressions are: *Could you elaborate on that?* and *Could you say some more about that?*

Unit 8.12   Getting Financial Backing
Language focus – questions for details

EXERCISE 1

Complete the questions below, using these words:

> clarification   particular   precisely
> exactly,   clear   specific

1. Are there any . . . . regulations we need to know about?
2. Could you be more . . . . , in particular, the amount of investment you expect from us?
3. We would also like some . . . . of the time scale you envisage.
4. . . . . how many people will be involved at our end?
5. What . . . . do you want? I mean, you haven't actually said what sort of return you're expecting.
6. One final point. We are not . . . . about the total amount of money needed to finance the project. Are you sure that there are no hidden costs here?

EXERCISE 2

Complete the sentences below using the following words:

> answer   simply   precise
> exact   need   concerned

a. Well, I'll be as . . . . as I can at this point. We anticipate that the whole project will be completed by the end of next year at the very latest.
b. As far as we are . . . . , everything has been cleared with customs and our lawyers see no problems.
c. If I can be more specific, what we . . . . is a deal which guarantees at least a 20% return on our investment.
d. Let me give you a categorical . . . . The total investment is £800,000 and we do not anticipate any extra costs.
e. To put it . . . . , we will need just two people – the Financial Director and the Project Manager.
f. If you want an . . . . figure, we would expect your investment to be no less than 25% of the total investment in the project, ie £200,000.

Now match the questions in Exercise 1 with the answers in Exercise 2.

1	2	3	4	5	6

Unit 8.13   Economic Indicators
Language focus – conditionals and trends

EXERCISE 1

Make complete sentences from the following notes:

1. if/price of oil/rise/price of petrol/usually/rise/too

. . . .

2. if/price of petrol/rise/transportation costs/also/rise

. . . .

3. if/transportation costs/increase/price of consumer goods/tend to go up

. . . .

4. when/price of consumer goods/go up/inflation rate/also/rise

. . . .

5. if/inflation rate/rise/bank/tend to raise/interest rates

. . . .

6. when/bank/raise/interest rates/value of pound/tend to/increase

. . . .

7. if/pound/rise/value of dollar/tend to fall

. . . .

8. if/value of dollar/fall/government/receive/less income/North Sea oil

. . . .

GRAMMAR NOTE

Look back and find a verb which is used 4 times in the examples to say what *usually* happens. It is a useful word in business, because it leaves you room to change your position a little in a discussion:

> *If a public holiday falls on a Thursday, people (tend to) take the Friday off and make a long weekend.*

EXERCISE 2

Decide whether these sentences represent a rise or a fall, and whether that rise or fall is small or large. The first one has been done for you as an example:

1. The price of oil shot up recently.   (*=large rise*)
2. Share prices on the London Stock Exchange slipped back a little yesterday.
3. The price of gold has slumped in recent weeks.
4. Shares soared when news of the takeover bid was made public.
5. There has been a slight increase in sales during the past six months.
6. The share price plunged when the takeover bid was rejected.
7. Commodity prices rallied slightly last week.
8. The pound was slightly stronger yesterday.

GRAMMAR NOTE

In conditional sentences, note that *will* is very rare in the *if*-clause.

Answer Key

1.1 Ex 1. 1. It's . . . there's 2. It's . . . There are 3. There'll be . . . It's 4. It's . . . there'll be 5. There's . . . It's 6. It's . . . there's 7. It's . . . there's 8. There are . . . it's . . . There's 9. there are 10. There's . . . It's 11. There's . . . it's 12. There's. . . It's 13. It's 14. There's
Ex 2. 1. O 2. M 3. M 4. T 5. O 6. O 7. T 8. O 9. O 10. M 11. M 12. O.

1.2 Ex 1. much: money / trouble many: customers / accounts much / many: change / time / development / opportunity. **Ex 2.** 1. much trouble 2. many changes 3. many opportunities 4. many changes / developments 5. much time 6. many customers
Ex 3. 1. Far 2. as 3. all 4. good 5. great 6. nowhere 7. Too 8. Too

1.3 1. a 2. b 3. c 4. a 5. b 6. a 7. c 8. a 9. b 10. b **Ex 2.** 1. Do you know how much it will cost? 2. When do you think they will sign the contract? 3. We'll fax you back as soon as possible with the details. 4. I'll try and phone again tomorrow. 5. When do you think the draft plan will be ready? 6. How long will it take to finish the project? 7. I'll send you further details later. 8. Will you please confirm this as soon as possible?

1.4 Ex 1. 1. d 2. a 3. d 4. c 5. e 6. a 7. d 8. c 9. b 10. e 11. d 12. b **Ex 2.** 1. I'm afraid they wouldn't agree to the price increase 2. They said they would prefer to renegotiate the contract. 3. A new agreement would also be better for us. 4. It would give us the chance to negotiate new terms. 5. We would be able to insert a penalty clause.

1.5 Ex 1. 1. Every day I receive as many as 100 faxes. 2. I also have to send 3. This usually takes up 4. I never have enough time 5. But I like my job very much. 6. I often meet 7. I have to travel abroad a lot as well. 8. About once a month I fly
Ex 2. 1. We have a board meeting once a month. 2. This takes place in the boardroom. 3. Board members always attend these meetings. 4. We usually spend most time on financial matters. 5. Sales and marketing are rarely discussed at these meetings. 6. Such matters are generally left to departmental meetings. 7. These are normally held weekly on Fridays. 8. We also have management meetings fairly often.

1.6 Ex 1. 1. in 2. on 3. on 4. in 5. out of 6. wide of 7. across 8. out of/in 9. to 10. under
Ex 2. 1. across the board 2. on the dot 3. in the same boat 4. on the ball 5. out of his depth 6. to the letter 7. under wraps 8. in the pipeline 9. out of touch 10. wide of

1.7 Ex 1. 1. from 2. out of 3. at 4. below 5. off 6. in 7. in 8. at 9. in 10. on
Ex 2. 1. below par 2. from scratch 3. at cross purposes 4. out of the question 5. on thin ice 6. at odds 7. in a rut 8. in a nutshell 9. off the record 10. in the balance

1.8 Ex 1. 1. in 2. at 3. in 4. in 5. for 6. in 7. at 8. for 9. out of 10. at 11. by 12. on 13. on 14. on **Ex 2.** 1. by chance 2. at a guess 3. out of the blue 4. in connection with 5. on equal terms 6. At first sight 7. for a change 8. in other words 9. in the long run 10. for the time being 11. in the dark 12. on the wrong foot 13. on the whole 14. at the deep end

1.9 1. a 2. a 3. b 4. b 5. b 6. b 7. b 8. b 9. a 10. b 11. a 12. a

1.10 Ex 1. 1. Don't forget 2. Don't delay 3. Don't forget 4. Don't mention 5. Do not obstruct 6. Don't expect 7. Don't miss 8. Do not enter 9. Do not use 10. Don't worry **Ex 2.** L 2, 3, 7; N 5, 8, 9; S 1, 4, 6, 10

1.11 1. range of colours 2. shadow of a doubt 3. shortage of spare parts 4. rate of growth 5. loss of income 6. lack of confidence 7. pace of development 8. flood of complaints 9. level of satisfaction 10. stroke of luck

1.12 Ex 1. 1. waste of time 2. time of arrival 3. member of my staff 4. token of goodwill 5. error of judgement 6. date of despatch 7. method of payment 8. team of (outside) experts 9. window of opportunity 10. portfolio of interests   **Ex 2.** 1. flood of danger 2. flow of time 3. trickle, stream, tide

1.13 1. look 2. disagreement 3. meeting 4. alternative 5. word 6. difficulty 7. time 8. appointment 9. break 10. day off 11. conversation 12. holiday 13. idea 14. headache 15. time 16. business 17. the steak 18. go 19. chance 20. doubt

1.14 Ex 1. 1. on with 2. across 3. over 4. down to 5. through 6. back to 7. round 8. together 9. at 10. by   **Ex 2.** 1. e 2. i 3. d 4. j 5. h 6. f 7. c 8. a 9. g 10. b

1.15 Ex 1. 1. do/are doing 2. make 3. make 4. made 5. are making 6. make . . . make 7. do 8. do 9. do 10. do 11. made 12. did 13. do 14. made 15. make 16. do . . . make 17. done . . . made 18. made . . . do   **Ex 2.** 1. make 2. do 3. make 4. do 5. make 6. do 7. do 8. make 9. do.

2.1 1. c 2. e 3. d 4. a 5. f 6. h 7. g 8. i 9. j 10. b

2.2 Ex 1. 1. I've mislaid 2. has jammed 3. has arrived 4. haven't come out 5. I've forgotten 6. I've missed 7. They've changed 8. We've run out of   **Ex 2.** a. give b. run off c. send d. give e. order f. check g. see h. get   **Ex 3.** 1. c 2. g 3. f 4. b 5. h 6. d 7. a 8. e

2.3 Ex 1. 1. Their machinery isn't very modern. 2. Their order processing isn't very quick. 3. The catalogue isn't very interesting. 4. We didn't get a j very warm reception. 5. We are not very satisfied . . . 6. We are not very happy . . . 7. We didn't make very much money on the deal. 8. He doesn't take very much interest . . . 9. There aren't many other options. 10. There isn't very much we can do.   **Ex 2.** 1. I can't put my hand on them at the moment. 2. I can't quite agree with you there. 3. We are not really interested at the moment.

2.4 1. takes . . . is taking 2. send . . . are sending 3. gives . . . are giving 4. use . . . are using 5. increase . . . are increasing 6. spend . . . are spending 7. try . . . are trying 8. borrow . . . aren't borrowing

2.5 Ex 1. 1. You'll have to delete some files. 2. You'll have to re-boot. 3. You'll have to upgrade. 4. You'll have to ring the helpline. 5. You'll have to back up.   **Ex 2.** 1. You mustn't forget to back up the file. 2. You must remember. 3. You have to load the new version before it works. 4. You mustn't use it until the new version is loaded. 5. You mustn't overload the memory by opening . . .

2.6 Ex 1. a. Why don't b. have to c. What about d. strongly advise e. you'd better f. were g. time h. could try; 1. d 2. g 3. f 4. a 5. c 6. e 7. h 8. b.   **Ex 2.** 2. better 4. don't you 6. could try 7. suppose 8. 'd better.

2.7 1. in front of 2. from 3. on top of 4. behind 5. out of 6. through 7. next to 8. against 9. over 10. between 11. all over 12. under

2.8 4, 5, 1, 2, 3

2.9 Ex 1. 1. kind/sort 2. though 3. work 4. same 5. must 6. Another 7. make 8. each 9. sort/kind 10. without 11. little 12. again 13. against 14. place 15. right.   **Ex 2.** In the first place, In fact, And don't forget, On the other hand, Having said that, The thing is.

2.10 1. Couldn't we . . . 2. Wouldn't it be . . . 3. Couldn't we . . . 4. Shouldn't we really . . . 5. Wouldn't July . . . 6. Shouldn't we . . . 7. Won't it be . . . 8. Haven't we got . . . 9. Couldn't we . . . 10. Aren't they . . .

2.11 1. Your order may be slightly delayed. 2. We would be grateful for your immediate reply. 3. There seems to be a mistake . . . 4. There seems to be the sum of £280 still outstanding. 5. We do not seem to have received . . . 6. We may have to introduce a slight increase . . . 7. You do not seem to have enclosed . . . 8. You may be experiencing a few . . . ; 1,6,8 = slightly/slight, few. The useful word is *seem*.

2.12 Ex 1. a. drawn up b. installed c. posted e. translated f. serviced h. decorated. 1. d 2. h 3. a 4. g 5. j 6. b 7. i 8. c 9. f 10. e.   **Ex 2.** 1. We had a lot of changes made to the contract. 2. First we had the penalty clauses removed. 3. Then we had the time limited extended. 4. Then we had a renewal option added. 5. Finally we had the whole contract re-translated.

3.1 Ex 1. 1. Are you here on business? 2. What line of business are you in? 3. What exactly do you do? 4. How long have you been doing that? 5. What did you do before that? 6. Does the job involve much travelling? 7. Whereabouts do you spend most of your time? 8. Is this your first visit to London? 9. When did you arrive? 10. How long are you here for?   **Ex 2.** 1. j 2. e 3. i 4. f 5. h 6. d 7. b 8. c 9. a 10. g

3.2 Ex 1. 1. I'm afraid I'm showing . . . 2. I'm afraid I'm preparing . . . 3. I'm afraid I'm presenting a report. 4. I'm afraid I'm having a day off . . . 5. I'm afraid I'm briefing . . . **Ex 2.** I was going to visit the trade fair, but now I'm briefing the Board. etc.

3.3 Ex 1. 1. g 2. e 3. a 4. i 5. f 6. b 7. h 8. j 9. d 10. c.   **Ex 2.** 1. Can I see the menu please? 2. I'm sorry but I didn't order this. 3. Would you like to see the wine list? 4. Could I have some more bread please? 5. Can I have the bill please? 6. Do you take Visa?

3.4 Ex 1. What time is the next train to Paris? 2. How long does it take to get there? 3. How much is a return? 4. Do I need a reservation? 5. Is there a restaurant car on the train? 6. Is it a direct train? 7. Can I reserve a seat for the return journey? 8. Where can I change some money? 9. Is there a cash dispenser near here? 10. What time does this office close?   **Ex 2.** . . . what time the next train to Paris is? 2. . . . how long it takes to get there? 3. . . . how much a return is? 4. . . . if/whether I need a reservation? 5. . . . if there is a restaurant car on the train? 6. . . . if/whether it is a direct train?

3.5 Ex 1. 1. along/down on 2. through, inside, to, on 3. at 4. on 6. to 7. through 8. straight 9. over/across 10. at.   **Ex 2.** 9, 5, 8, 1, 2, 4, 10, 3, 7, 6.

3.6 Para 1. 1. even fly 2. never fly 3. usually prefer 3, 2, 1. **Para 2.** 1. always stay 2. also trying 3. often run up 4. are now encouraging; 1, 3, 4, 2. **Para 3.** 1. frequently indicates 2. are currently introducing 3. rarely succeed; 2, 3, 1.

3.7 1. g 2. e 3. a 4. b 5. i 6. c 7. f 8. d 9. h

4.1 Ex 1. 1. three and a half hours 2. one thousand two hundred . . . 3. seven minutes past 4. BA eight five eight 5. five o'clock or five pm 6. by, not times 7. three hundred people 8. four point five six nine 9. two pounds fifty   **Ex 2.** 1. one and a half hours/an hour and a half 2. two point oh seven five 3. double oh double four one four two four double two double three double four. 4. eleven fifty/ten to twelve 5. thirty-three point three percent 6. a hundred and twenty-five 7. BA eight five six 8. GB = the twelfth of November, US = the eleventh of December 9. two thousand and one 10. a hundred kilometres per hour

4.2 Ex 1. 1. malpress at aol dot com 2. http slash www dot comm col dot co dot UK **Ex 2.** 1. number seventy five stroke twelve C 2. sixty-two pounds per person per day 3. marked asterisk carry a twenty percent 4. one pound equals approximately one dollar sixty-five 5. six point five million pounds per annum 6. three metres by four 7. thirty-two dash twenty-six dash forty-two 8. eighteen degrees Centigrade

4.3 1. fell 2. have been rising 3. have risen 4. was, has risen 5. have increased 6. has shrunk 7. grew 8. have gone up 9. fell 10. was

4.4 1. g 2. i 3. f 4. d 5. a 6. h 7. b 8. e 9. c.

93

4.5 Ex 1. 1. twice as much as 2. almost as much as 3. far bigger than 4. slightly cheaper than 5. much more expensive than 6. much less expensive than 7. more than twice as expensive as 8. not nearly as much as.   **Ex 2.** 2. is twice as much as 3. not nearly as much as 4. far bigger than 5. much more expensive than 6. much less expensive than 7. more than twice as expensive as 8. slightly cheaper than

4.6 1. d 2. e 3. g 4. h 5. a 6. i 7. f 8. c 9. b

4.7 1. d 2. i 3. l 4. m 5. j 6. e 7. f 8. b 9. n 10. h 11. a 12. c 13. g 14. k

4.8 Ex 1. a. region b. between c. around d. give or take e. roughly f. less g. towards h. not more than   **Ex 2.** 1. e 2. h 3. c 4. f 5. d 6. b 7. a 8. g

5.1 Ex 1. 1. writes 2. addresses 3. turns 4. travel 5. use 6. converts . . . read 7. checks 8. reads.   **Ex 2.** 1. E-mail is used to send messages quickly and efficiently. 2. Messages are sent via a modem. 3. Messages can be sent to anyone with a compatible system. 4. E-mail is often used by multi-national companies. 5. A lot of time is saved in this way. 6. Efficiency has been improved by introducing e-mail for communication.

5.2 Ex 1. 1. is made up 2. is made 3. is powered 4. is operated 5. is used 6. are taken 7. is transmitted 8. is processed 9. are displayed 10. are stored   **Ex 2.** 1. a pair of scissors 2. transparencies 3. paper-clips 4. credit cards 5. bottle opener 6. mobile phone.

5.3 Ex 1. 1. A lot of companies are now targeting Eastern Europe. 2. Some Eastern European economies are growing very quickly. 3. Numerous foreign companies are investing in these countries. 4. Many companies are trying to establish joint ventures. 5. Some Eastern European currencies are now rising in value. 6. Some companies are producing goods under licence in these countries. 7. The quality of domestic goods is improving. 8. The quality of hotels and other services is also improving. 9. Industrial output is rising again. 10. Unfortunately, the unemployment rate is also rising. **Ex 2.** 1. establish 2. domestic 3. grow 4. unemployment 5. produce 6. rise 7. quality 8. output

5.4 3, 6, 9, 1, 7, 2, 10, 5, 8, 4.

5.5 1. I'd like to start 2. To begin with 3. For example 4. Furthermore 5. on the other hand 6. Apart from this 7. As far as price is concerned 8. however 9. Last but not least

5.6 1. e 2. c 3. i 4. h 5. b 6. j 7. f 8. a 9. d 10. g

5.7 1. i 2. f 3. j 4. k 5. a 6. g 7. b 8. c 9. e 10. l 11. h 12. d

5.8 Ex 1. a. had to, close had to be discussed, have to consolidate, have to turn our attention; b. have expanded, has been very steady, had ever closed, have managed, have decided; c. has three separate divisions; d. had some difficulty, had a series, have a large share, have any problems   **Ex 2.** 1. f 2. d 3. e 4. b 5. a 6. c

5.9 Ex 1. 1. e 2. d 3. b 4. f 5. a 6. c.   **Ex 2.** 1. mention 2. offer 3. the guarantee 4. to complete 5. differ from 6. under 7. achieve 8. clarify

6.1 Ex 1. 1. someone 2. back 3. please 4. message 5. called 6. again 7. line 8. try 9. speak 10. catch   **Ex 2.** a. soon b. see c. get d. course e. anyone f. 'll g. hear h. back i. wait j. like. 1. e 2. c 3. b 4. j 5. a 6. f 7. i 8. h 9. g 10. d

6.2 1. written, confirm 2. moment, try 3. know, let 4. rather, make 5. back, get 6. speak, see 7. information, put 8. afraid, be 9. answer, need

6.3 1. Can you give me your name please? 2. How would you like to pay? 3. What type of card is it? 4. What is the full mailing address? 5. What would you like to order? 6. What is the card number? 7. What is the expiry date? 8. Is there any reference (you'd like me to put)? 9. How would you like the goods dispatched? 10. Could I have a telephone number (in case of any problems)?

6.4 Ex 1. 1. b 2. d 3. a 4. c   **Ex 2.** 1. would 2. should 3. Could 4. will 5. will 6. should 7. Could 8. would

6.5 Ex 1. 1. Unfortunately, we are . . . 2. We will probably be . . . 3. We have recently been . . . 4. We are currently reviewing . . . 5. Fortunately we noticed . . . 6. Apparently it was . . . 7. Our systems usually ensure . . . 8. The goods have just . . . 9. We frequently use . . . 10. In general this means . . . Words which describe the whole sentence come in the initial position. **Ex 2.** 1. I have just . . . 2. You are probably . . . 3. I always try . . . 4. I usually answer . . . 5. I normally send . . . 6. Unfortunately, our . . .

7.1 1. have had 2. has helped 3. started 4. employed 5. has grown 6. has grown 7. worked 8. had 9. have changed 10. moved 11. faced 12. won 13. took on 14. invested 15. have gone 16. have expanded 17. strengthened 18. have resulted 19. has enabled 20. represented

7.2 1. there had been 2. had not been 3. had been 4. were 5. had supplied 6. had arrived 7. had promised 8. charged 9. was 10. were offering 11. could 12. would 13. reduced 14. offered 15. guaranteed

7.3 Ex 1. 1. They asked us when the materials would be ready. 2. They also asked how much they would cost. 3. The purchasing manager asked how we usually ship our goods. 4. They also asked what the payment terms were. 5. They asked when the last contract had finished. 6. They also wanted to know when the contract would start. 7. They also asked if the price was fixed. 8. They asked if the contract was renewable.   **Ex 2.** They asked: 1. when the contract started. 2. how many companies were involved. 3. if there was a penalty clause. 4. how many units we could supply each month. 5. how the goods would be shipped. 6. how much discount we could offer. 7. if the agreement was flexible. 8. if we could guarantee the terms.

7.4 Ex 1. 1. offered, (would) reflect 2. have been, have run out of 3. produce, produce 4. are looking at, reduce, are paying 5. will accept, will sign 6. was introduced, had, discussed 7. offer 8. have/had suffered 9. is experiencing **Ex 2.** 3, 6, 9, 4, 8, 1, 2, 7, 5

7.5 Ex 1. 1. had been circulated 2. was agreed 3. was reported 4. was decided 5. was proposed 6. was reached 7. has been denied 8. was adjourned.   **Ex 2.** 1. Smiths is regarded as one of the UK's . . . 2. The information was obtained from . . . 3. The budget was cleared . . . 4. It was agreed unanimously.

8.1 1. h 2. a 3. c 4. d 5. f 6. e 7. g 8. b. Search. a. 2, 3; b. start by, followed by, look forward to

8.2 Ex 1. 1. of benefit to 2. co-operate with 3. as a basis for 4. in favour of 5. at this point 6. limited to 7. the possibility of 8. at some 9. on this basis   **Ex 2.** 10. stand on 11. in a position 12. preferable to 13. opposed to 14. present circumstances 15. at this stage 16. of benefit to 17. As far as 18. in favour of

8.3 Ex 1. 1. g 2. b 3. c 4. h 5. d 6. a 7. f 8. e   **Ex 2.** Fantastic, essential, furious, useless, astonished, fascinating, amazing, exhausted

8.4 1. short 2. way 3. simply 4. nutshell 5. word 6. words 7. bluntly 8. frankly; 1. e 2. a 3. f 4. h 5. c 6. g 7. d 8. b

8.5 Ex 1. There isn't much we can do about it. 2. There's no alternative. 3. There's been a change to the programme. 4. There were no seats left. 5. There might not have been room for everybody. 6. There wasn't enough time to finish yesterday. 7. There's no way we'll be there on time. 8. There'll be trouble when they find out what's happened.

Ex 2. a-4, b-3, c-5, d-6, e-2, f-1, g-8, h-7   **Ex 3.** 1. Are there any other points to consider? 2. Have there been any calls for me? 3. Is there anything else we need to talk about? 4. Will there be any problem with finance?

8.6 1. e 2. f 3. a 4. j 5. i 6. c 7. g 8. b 9. h 10. d

8.7 Ex 1. 1. satisfy 2. excluding/rejecting 3. choose 4. put 5. examine 6. reach 7. brings 8. exclude/reject 9. seems 10. give   **Ex 2.** 5, 8, 1, 10, 2, 7, 3, 9, 6, 4

8.8 1. f 2. c 3. a 4. d 5. g 6. h 7. e 8. b.   **Ex 2.** 2. I firmly believe that 3. It is absolutely essential to 4. The crux of the matter is 5. I really must stress that 6. It's impossible to over-emphasize the importance of

8.9 Ex 1. 1. unable 2. bottom 3. up to a point 4. position 5. final 6. moving 7. clear 8. unacceptable 9. limit 10. leave   **Ex 2.** 1. offer 2. meet 3. deal 4. make 5. stick to 6. offer 7. price 8. negotiations 9. offer

8.10 Ex 1. a. in, in b. on, from, to c. on, in d. with, with e. over, In f. on, in g. on, from h. with, with   **Ex 2.** 1. c 2. e 3. f 4. a 5. d 6. g 7. h 8. b

8.11 Ex 1. 2. dissatisfied 3. helpful 5. satisfied 6. suprised, specific 7. appalling 9. happy 10. frank, impressed 11. unreliable   **Ex 2.** 5, 12, 4, 10, 2, 7, 6, 8, 3, 11, 1, 9

8.12 Ex 1. 1. particular 2. specific 3. clarification 4. Exactly 5. precisely 6. clear. **Ex 2.** a. precise b. concerned c. need d. answer e. simply f. exact; 1b 2f 3a 4e 5c 6d

8.13 Ex 1. 1. If the price of oil rises, the price of petrol usually rises too. 2. If the price of petrol rises, transportation costs also rise. 3. If transportation costs increase, the price of consumer goods tends to go up. 4. When the price of consumer goods goes up, the inflation rate also rises. 5. If the inflation rate rises, the bank tends to raise interest rates. 6. When the bank raises interest rates, the value of the pound tends to increase. 7. If the pound rises, the value of the dollar tends to fall. 8. If the value of the dollar falls, the government receives less income from North Sea oil.   **Ex 2.** 2. small fall 3. large fall 4. large rise 5. small rise 6. large fall 7. small rise 8. small rise